BREATH OF HEAVEN

MANIFESTING
GOD'S WAY

USING THE LAWS OF
THE BIBLE AND BRAIN SCIENCE TO
CREATE AN ABUNDANTLY BLESSED LIFE
BY ERICA ELLIOTT, MS

ISBN: 978-1-968061-37-1

Table of Contents

Foreword

By Lisa Sylvester Wong, MS, Christian Counselor, Soundmind Counseling, LLC

My relationship with Erica Elliott began over thirty years ago. We met as colleagues and quickly became lifelong friends. From the very beginning, Erica stood out—not just as a professional, but as a mentor, a woman of unwavering faith, and a source of encouragement and wisdom. She was the one who inspired me to complete my degree in counseling, and she has continued to inspire me—and many others—ever since.

My experience with Erica includes attending various workshops she led on mental health, counseling, neuroscience, and Christian topics. She was the first to expose me to how to effectively run a successful public workshop—an experience that deeply influenced my understanding of community healing and outreach. Her ability to blend compassion with practical tools is just one of the many qualities that make her work so impactful.

I have had the privilege of knowing Erica both personally and professionally. Her integrity, compassion, and relentless desire to see people healed and walking in their God-given identity radiate in all she does. She carries a unique gift: the ability to unite the rigor of science with the breath of the spirit. *Breath of Heaven: Manifesting God's Way* is a stunning reflection of that gift. This book invites readers to harness the power of brain science—not as a worldly tool for self-help, but as a sacred pathway to transformation through God's design. Erica masterfully introduces manifestation and visualization techniques supported by neuroscience, showing how the mind can be renewed and reprogrammed in alignment with biblical truth. In doing so, she reminds us that recovery is not just possible, it's promised, when we think the way God calls us to think.

Scripture tells us in Proverbs 23:7, "*As a man thinketh in his heart, so is he.*" Erica builds upon this timeless wisdom, demonstrating how our thoughts shape our reality—biologically, emotionally, and spiritually. She shows us how to rewire destructive patterns and align our thinking with God's Will. Through practical exercises, revelatory teaching, and scientific insight, this book equips you to not only believe in God's promises but to actively manifest them in your life. This message is bold, timely, and desperately needed. *Breath of Heaven* will speak to the wounded, the seeking, the stuck, and the spiritually hungry. It will also speak to counselors, leaders, and anyone longing for deeper tools to bring healing and wholeness to others.

My hope is that you just read this book and that you experience it. Let its truth sink in. Let its wisdom challenge you. Let its Spirit breathe life into you. Because healing is possible. Renewal is within reach. And heaven is already reaching for you.

With Love, Lisa Sylvester Wong

Foreword

By Misty Cowan, MS, LPC, Counselor, Rula.com Therapist

I have known the author of this book as a dear friend and sister, but also as a therapist whom I aspired to be more like each day for over 10 years. She knew scripture and the Bible as events would arise in my life, and just knew exactly how to share God's Word over my mind and do exercises to bring me peace for me and my family. Over the years, I heard her doing these visualization practices with me and mindfulness, as well as teaching me about the power of positivity and the mind, using scripture, of course. For example, my son has struggled with a drug and alcohol addiction, and for a time, I was allowing it to ruin my life and affect my thoughts, my choices, and my ability to be a therapist myself. I had so much self-doubt as a mother who had a son making such bad decisions. As a therapist, I could not help or impact anyone in a positive way anymore. I was also lost in reading the Bible and had no idea growing up in church that I did not know how to manifest or actually pray. I grew up praying prayers that you memorize, and it wasn't until I wanted more and felt like I needed more food in church that I sought out to learn what was missing in my life. I needed the Holy Spirit. It was in this book, *Breath of Heaven Manifesting God's Way*, and Erica's support that I found how to pray meaningfully with intent and purpose. I found that I was speaking curses of negative thoughts into my life and about my son. I also found that in scripture, she says we find a "Well Spring," this water we need to feed our soul. In His Word, He tells us, "Rejoice in the Lord always, I will say it again: Rejoice! Let your gentleness be evident to all. The Lord is near. Do not be anxious about anything, but in every situation, by prayer and repetition, with thanksgiving, present your requests to God and the peace of God which transcends all understanding, will guard your hearts and minds in Christ Jesus." Wait, is this saying I am not trusting God if I am anxious? That my worry doesn't work? That peace is right here if I ask for it? Then I read more, and I see, "Finally, my brothers and sisters, whatever is true, whatever is pure, whatever is lovely, whatever is admirable—if anything is excellent or praiseworthy—think about such things" (Philippians 4). So, I learned that I was speaking out negatively and vomiting on my son all day and all night to everyone I knew until I burned my own light out. I was empty until I filled myself back up with the water of the word. Erica leads you through a journey of self-discovery of the power and tools we all hold within ourselves and our minds. To manifest, I thought for the longest time, was using energy from the world and was bad, or scary, or evil. What we do not know, we cannot understand until we learn about everything. So, I continued to read and learn and understand that my daily prayers did not have to be generic but could be specific. So, one day after I read Erica say that we can use a META PRAYER. Before I was a learned manifestor, at that time I was still suffering from bouts of anxiousness caused by my own negative thought patterns and I would use this saying: "May I have Peace, May I have Joy, May I have Wisdom" until I felt better, resetting my compassion center and ultimately giving it to God. Then, I would say for the person who I felt hurt by, "May they have Peace, may they feel Love, May they have Joy, and May they have Wisdom." This helped tremendously for me to rebuild my relationship with my son and feel love versus shame, guilt, and anger. The next phase, I began to get excited about this new power I had to teach, so I started to guide people through imagery of imagining the life they wanted and how to use this imagery to manifest it. How to use God's Word as water and reshape your thoughts to bring peace and joy. Ultimately, I sat down and said, "What do I want my life to look like? What do I want for my son in his daily thought life?" So, I wrote down daily affirmations for him and myself. I invite peace and joy into my life. I invite money to come to me in expected and unexpected ways. I will be confident in my decision-making. I will only look for and speak out the good. For my son, a few of his affirmations were: "I believe in myself today," "Today, I will look for the good in my life," "I can do hard things," "I can forgive myself for mistakes," "I can ask for help," "With Faith, I can move a mountain." Then I began to realize this positive energy that began to flow from within as I felt more confident and powerful with believing that I had peace and joy, and God wanted me to be blessed and feel abundance in life. I believe that this book has helped transform not only my life but also my daily sessions with my clients. I use this in daily practice to help people become the best version of themselves, and if it aligns with God's principles, that is the life He wants for you, and you begin to bloom and see the fruits of His blessings all around you. I am not a writer and was reluctant to share my journey with others, but the power of transformation should be granted to everyone. One of the most powerful verses in manifestation is Mark 11:24, which states, *"Therefore I tell you, whatever you ask for in prayer, believe it that you have received it, and it will be yours."* Mathew 17:20, *"Truly, I tell you, if you have faith as small as a mustard seed, you can say to this mountain, move from here to there, and it will move."* I can use scripture to lead people in their relationships with Jesus. I can pray intently over my family, and I can teach others how to manifest the life they so badly desire by learning how our brain works, as well as skills to align our requests with God's way. *A Breath of Heaven* was truly a Breath of Heaven for me, for I was desperate for Heaven to meet me right now, and now I walk by faith, not by sight.

Sincerely,
Misty Cowan

Foreword

By Carmen K. Maendel, BA in Arts and Business, Special Education, and a Certification in Speech & Language Pathology, Certified Fitness Trainer, CNS, PN1, DNA Testing and Analysis, CO-Owner of Nate's Property Maintenance LLC, Bestselling National and International Author, and Revered Speaker

Erica Elliott truly is a "Breath of Heaven." She guides you along a beautiful journey of self-awareness and how to attain and maintain a healthy mindset.

This book outlines key points on how to live life with a healthy mindset.

Erica dives deep into the human brain to reveal the ways the neurological system processes and stores information. She shows how those undesirable thoughts and pathways can be rewired for a life full of abundance. Erica walks you through the process of how to harness the power of brain science to manifest your goals and aspirations in life.

She uses visualization techniques, affirmation, and crushing limiting beliefs to help elevate you to a whole new level. I believe this little book is a love letter from God to all those who pick it up and read it in its entirety. This is encouragement to all of us as we are walking along our own journeys and paths God lays out for us.

It is the assurance that we are not alone, and we are being gently guided through life, similarly to the poem "Footprints." God does not promise that challenging things won't happen in our lives; however, He does promise to be right there beside us to help us through those challenging moments of our lives.

Erica uses interactive questions and activities that cause you to re-evaluate and take action in your own life. There is scripture and encouragement woven throughout this whole book, with questions for reflection and deep thought.

Erica's passion for the work she does with her clients, daily, shines through in this amazing guidebook to creating an abundant and blessed life for yourself.

This book truly is captivating and illuminating!

I have also had the pleasure to hear Erica speak in a public setting, and her passion flows freely from her heart, out of her mouth, with ease. I highly recommend this book, and Erica is an expert in her field of brain science and counseling with her company, Counselor and Brain Health Coach— WarriorHeart Healing Hearts (Erica Elliott, MS, LPC).

Sincerely,
Carmen Maendel

Foreword

By Elishama Joy, AA in Liberal Arts, and Coach and Intuitive Quantum Healing Guide

Some people come into your life and change everything. For me, Erica has been one of those people. A powerful, divinely appointed soul I couldn't have gotten to where I am without.

Our connection began with simple morning meditations, but it quickly blossomed into a soul-level friendship. Over the past nine months, Erica has walked beside me through some of the darkest, most difficult moments of my life—not with judgment, but with unwavering love, deep compassion, and incredible wisdom.

What makes Erica's guidance so powerful is that it's not just words on paper and knowledge recited—it's lived. With multiple degrees and over 25 years of practicing with countless clients and helping them transform permanently, she doesn't simply teach these tools; she embodies them. She's walked through her own shadows, transmuted her own pain, and emerged with a deep-rooted compassion and a fire to help humanity heal at the root. She lives what she teaches, and her integrity and intuition shine through in every interaction.

She taught me how to navigate my own healing without shame—to witness myself with grace, to honor every part of me, and to transform pain into power through energetic clearing, inner child healing, and tools that truly work.

The practices and insights in this book are the same ones that helped me shift not just my mindset, but my entire way of being and the lens I see life through—even when I wasn't showing up perfectly or practicing daily. That's the beauty of Erica's approach: it's not about perfection; it's about permission—to heal, to grow, to manifest, and to live a life aligned with who you truly are.

She helped me understand that abundance is so much more than money—it's gratitude, peace, love, freedom, purpose, and self-love. This book breaks down the how and the why behind manifesting real, lasting transformation. And Erica doesn't just teach it—she lives it. She is a walking example of what's possible when we align with God/Source/Creator within us and remember our power.

If you're holding this book in your hands, it's not by accident. Trust that you're being guided to exactly what your soul needs next. Let Erica's words, her heart, and her tools support you the way they've supported me.

With deep love and gratitude,
Elishama Joy

Foreword

By Agnieszka Pearl Der, BA, Senior Account Payable and Payroll Specialist for Risk & Insurance Education Alliance, and Life Coach

This is not just a book. It's a remembering.

When I first began meditating with Erica, I didn't know what I was walking into. All I knew was that something in me was tired of carrying it all.

> *The trying.*

> *The performing.*

The pretending I had to know what I was doing to be worthy of rest, love, or miracles. But week after week, in the quiet space she held, something began to soften.

> *She didn't push.*

> *She didn't perform.*

> *She embodied.*

Erica doesn't teach from a script—she teaches from presence. She doesn't tell you what to believe—she holds you while your own knowing returns.

She led us through meditations that felt less like practices and more like homecomings.

> *Home to the breath.*

> *Home to the now.*

Home to the holy truth that we don't have to understand in order to surrender.

> *Six months in her space changed me.*

Not through lightning bolts or grand revelations.

But through love.

Quiet. Steady. Wildly intelligent love.

She taught me that sending love—to others, yes, but especially to myself—isn't selfish. It's sacred.

She reminded me that letting go isn't weakness—it's worship. That we don't manifest by chasing, striving, or fixing.

We manifest by remembering who we are... and whose we are. This book is the transmission of all that.

It weaves together the mystery of God with the clarity of brain science.

It speaks to both your sacred logic and your wild heart.

It's not here to tell you how to manifest.

It's here to wake up the part of you that already knows.

And if you let it, this book will hold you like Erica does—with grace, humor, deep truth, and the unwavering presence of someone who has walked through fire and came back radiant.

This book is a love letter to your becoming.

To your softness.

To your co-creation with the Divine.

I'm forever changed because of Erica.

Because of her courage to live what she teaches.

Because of her willingness to be a vessel instead of a guru.

Because of the way she helped me remember—

I don't need to be perfect to be powerful.

I don't need to know to let go.

And I don't need to do it alone.

So here you are.

Holding these pages.

Maybe feeling cracked open. Curious. Ready.

Welcome, beloved. You're not late. You're right on divine time.

Read slowly. Breathe deep.

Let yourself be loved.

With reverence, laughter, and the fiercest kind of gratitude,

Agnieszka Pearl Der

Author's Biography

Erica Elliott is an inspiring and multifaceted leader in the realms of literature, entrepreneurship, and community service. A celebrated author, achieved the prestigious status of National and International Bestseller, with additional titles and to be released soon. Erica continues to carve her niche in the literary world, published in several magazines, while captivating audiences as a sought-after international speaker.

In her collaboration with Fenix TV Studios, Erica is featured in a docuseries spotlighting women authors and entrepreneurs. She is also on the brink of launching her own TV series, *The Masterpiece You Are*, which promises to inspire by unraveling the mystery of you.

Erica's diverse background includes an impressive 12 ½ years of service in the military as a Behavioral Science Specialist and Medic. Her dedication and excellence earned her numerous awards, including the Army Achievement Medal, Humanitarian Service Medal, and Oklahoma Alfred P. Murrah Service Medal. Beyond her military service, Erica is a published model, songwriter, and commercial actress, and has participated in various photocons and fashion shows.

She has extensive experience in ministry, ranging from singles director to music minister, and has worked with children and youth as well. Erica's community service expands throughout her life as a CASA volunteer and now provides free women's empowerment workshops to help women heal and find community support.

She is retired from the Federal Government, where she worked as a trauma counselor with combat veterans and their families, and has been recognized with numerous awards for her invaluable contributions.

Erica earned her Master's in Counseling Psychology from Southern Nazarene University. Graduating with honors in both Graduate and Undergraduate—

Cum Laude and Phi Chi Honor Society. She is a Licensed Counselor and holds multiple certifications, including Certified Brain Health Coach, Certified Mental Health Integrative Medicines Professional, Certified Clinical Trauma Professional, Certified Thought Field Therapist, and MYS Certified Coach, boasting over 35 years of experience in the field. She has been nominated for Who's Who in Business Leaders.

As the visionary founder of WarriorHeart Healing Hearts, LLC, Erica delivers exceptional services while also offering free community support initiatives aimed at uplifting and encouraging others to reach their full potential. She helps people clear the mess to discover their Masterpiece. Her commitment to empowering individuals is further demonstrated through previous work as a presenter teaching communication entrepreneurship skills in Swaziland, Africa.

Adding a touch of adventure to her story, Erica and her husband bought a yacht, completed coast guard safety training, and spent a year traveling the ocean while writing her first book, journeying from Kemah, Texas, to various parts of Florida and eight beautiful islands in the Bahamas. Besides taking the helm of the boat, she has also taken lessons towards her pilot's license.

As a devoted wife, mother, and grandmother, Erica Elliott exemplifies the extraordinary ability of women to excel in multiple roles and pursue their passions with unwavering determination. Her life's journey serves as a powerful reminder of the strength and resilience inherent in embracing one's unique path with God as her Pilot.

Introduction

Long ago, a gentle divine whisper awakened my longing to write this book and share my journey. At first, I hesitated, wrestling with the vulnerability of opening my heart to the world. Though I have always aspired to be a vessel for God's Will, telling my story felt overwhelming, especially in a landscape often rife with misunderstandings and heated debates about faith. Yet the persistent nudges from God echoed the struggles faced by figures like Moses and Jonah, compelling me to confront this calling. I want to be frank here, God clearly showed me how many people are trying to understand manifestation and delving into areas that first seem to be magnificent and magical, but as time goes on, those people find themselves in a darker feeling of separation from God. I will also spend some time sharing a bit more of these insights of what God has shown me.

I needed to approach this task with care, especially considering the diverse paths my family members have taken over the years. Despite a challenging and, at times, traumatic childhood, I hold a deep respect for my family, recognizing they did the best they could with the understanding they had at the time. The transformation within my family is profound and far removed from the past I once knew.

When I speak of the gift of manifestation, I mean it sincerely—not just as a personal treasure but as a universal blessing for everyone. As I even use the word universal, the meaning here is truly that there are God-ordained laws, which I will explain more in depth in the following chapters, that are laws no different than Newton's Law of Gravity. No matter what, it applies to all. In these pages, I will recount how God guided me in discovering the art of manifestation as a child, illuminating a path that I hope will encourage you to deepen your relationship with God. I pray this book leads you toward a life filled with purpose, joy, and abundant blessings.

If you find yourself questioning God's love or presence in your life, know that you are not alone. I, too, have wrestled with such doubts. Throughout my years of working with countless individuals who have faced pain from religious experiences or felt abandoned in their darkest moments, I have come to understand that these things come from people, not God, and the misunderstandings of how God works. I hope this book clarifies and reassures you that God truly loves you and desires your best.

In sharing my journey, the experiences of others, and the wisdom found in God's Word, I aim to unveil the truths and principles that can guide us toward manifesting a life filled with positivity and blessings. As well as understanding more about how we can block those blessings and how to get clear of those blocks to blessings.

For more than three decades, I have devoted my life to guiding individuals on their journey toward healing and personal growth as a licensed counselor, coach, and speaker. Throughout these years, I have assisted thousands in overcoming challenges and past traumas, empowering them to embrace a life filled with healing, purpose, and joy. My heartfelt aspiration is that this book serves as a source of healing for you, fostering a deeper connection with God as you discover how to manifest a blessed and abundant life in alignment with His ways.

I wish to express my commitment to representing God with the utmost respect and sharing the insights and concepts He has imparted to me. It is important to note that the teachings in this book are not intended to replace healthy counseling, coaching, or guidance; rather, they are meant to complement your pursuit of God's wisdom and wise counsel. The principles outlined in this book do not guarantee that you will achieve the same manifestations as I or others, as each person's life path, purpose, and beliefs are unique. However, when applied correctly, these laws and guidance can indeed assist you in manifesting a blessed life.

Motivated by a deep sense of purpose, I felt compelled to write this book to help you understand how your brain operates concerning neuroscience and how this science affirms biblical teachings. We will also dive into the stuck points our brain can have due to life's teachings and events. Within these pages, you will discover how the Bible offers us a framework for manifesting a life of abundance and personal stories from my own experiences. Additionally, I have included exercises designed to strengthen your mind, clear blocks and limiting beliefs, and equip you with tools for improved mental health and manifestation skills. I am truly grateful for your presence here, and I pray that your journey is enriched with insights, growth, love, and abundant blessings as you embrace your potential to manifest a life of beauty and purpose. In the work God has called me to, I help people clear the mess to discover their Masterpiece. For years, one of the insights and inspirations I share is... You were created as a Masterpiece, and sometimes we need to clear the mess to discover the Masterpiece God intended you to be. I believe God has shown me that we were all born a Masterpiece, yet in this world, we may lose sight of that for different reasons, as I will share more about it in the depths of these pages.

About four years ago, my life took a dramatic turn when I contracted COVID-19. During that challenging time, I found myself searching for ways to heal my body, revisiting the practices that had previously helped me manifest healing in my life, and helping others to do the same. In my pursuit of understanding, I turned to God and asked Him to guide me in the manifestation of healing, not only in my body and mind, but also in other areas of life. As I sought His wisdom, He began to reveal various places in my life where I could manifest change to create a healing space.

I started implementing many tools that you will discover in this book—some of which I developed through continuous learning and research, while others I learned from things I encountered over the years, from various books, teaching, mentors, and training. Each of these tools has been invaluable to me and the clients I've worked with over the years, and I sincerely hope they serve you just as well. There were moments of deep struggle when I was still very sick and desperately pleading with God to show me a path to healing. I vividly remember times when I thought, "God, I don't know how much longer I can endure this." I battled excruciating daily migraines and fatigue like I had never experienced before. Each time I cried out to God, He answered. Sometimes, it was in clear guidance, and other times, it guided me to a path through learning.

Through this journey, God taught me how to utilize the very tools you'll read about in this book. Today, I can say I am in significantly better health than four years ago. However, I want to be transparent, and I am still navigating some of my health journey... having dealt with complete adrenal fatigue and autoimmune issues that arose after my illness has meant creating a space for healing. Many of those challenges have improved tremendously, with some even completely healed.

Throughout this process, I discovered that I had been manifesting the life I always dreamed of but had never taken the time to invest in creating. As God guided me in using these tools more effectively, my husband and I embarked on an incredible adventure. We sold everything, became debt-free, accumulated around one million dollars in assets, built our dream home, purchased a motor yacht, and traveled for one year from Kemah, Texas, to most of Florida and across eight islands in the Bahamas. Since writing the first publication, I have had the joy of traveling to more countries and writing more books. In these past few years, I have experienced more joy and connection than I ever thought possible, forging wonderful friendships along the way. Literally clearing more of my own mess to live a life of the Masterpiece God created me to be. I know that as you dive in and draw closer to God, He desires the same for your life. Masterpiece is not an ego-centered, narcissistic, better-than-someone-else state. It is embracing the amazing creation God created us to be, to not only heal ourselves and live in blessings with God as our pilot in life, but also to help others do the same.

I owe it all to God for teaching me how to manifest more clearly and deeply. This gift is not exclusive to me; it is available to anyone willing to put in the effort and seek God's guidance. You, too, can see your dreams come to life in ways you never thought possible. Immense miracles as they unfold in your life, and that is my heartfelt prayer and belief for you as you embark on this journey to create a truly blessed and manifested life with God as your pilot. I pray you keep an open mind as you tap into these tools and let God teach you how to have an abundant, incredible, and blessed life so you can share your blessings and journey with others, too. Let's begin!

Embrace the Power of Manifestation

Embark on a transformative journey that intertwines the enduring wisdom of the Bible with the latest discoveries in brain science, all while weaving in my personal narrative. This book is designed to guide you in manifesting a life filled with joy and fulfillment. Whether you are a newcomer to the idea of manifestation of your deepest prayers and dreams coming true or have been delving into it for a while, you'll find practical tools, inspiring insights, and actionable strategies designed to harmonize your thoughts, beliefs, and actions with your highest aspirations and divine purpose. Are you seeking to attract abundance, nurturing relationships, exciting adventures, vibrant health, healing from life's tragedies, or delightful surprises? If so, this book is tailored for you.

Understanding Manifestation

Manifestation is the art of transforming your desires and goals into reality by harnessing the power of focused thought, prayer, biblical teaching, unwavering belief, and aligned action. It transcends mere wishful or magical thinking and, instead, involves utilizing connecting with God, the strength of your mind, spiritual principles, and faith to craft the life you envision. Within these pages, you will discover how your thoughts and beliefs influence and shape your reality and learn how to intentionally guide them toward manifesting positive results. As I show you how to clear the mess and discover the Masterpiece God created you to be.

The Power of Biblical Principles

The Bible is a profound reservoir of wisdom and guidance, inspiring and transforming lives for centuries. By weaving biblical principles into your manifestation practice, you anchor your journey in faith and divine truth. The scriptures provide deep insights into the power of God through belief, the significance of positive thinking, and the transformative effects of prayer and meditation. As you delve into these principles, you will discover how engaging with God and the Word can lead to remarkable transformations in your life.

Insights from Brain Science

Recent breakthroughs in neuroscience have deepened our understanding of brain function and how we can leverage this knowledge to enhance our lives. Remarkably, the principles found in God's Word align with findings in brain science. Concepts like neuroplasticity, mindfulness, affirmations, journaling, meditation, and positive visualization are scientifically validated techniques that can rewire our brains for success and well-being. This book intricately blends these scientific insights with biblical wisdom, offering a holistic approach to manifestation that is both practical and spiritually enriching.

What You Will Discover

In the following chapters, you will find a comprehensive guide to manifestation enriched with interactive questions, exercises, and real-life testimonies. You will learn to:

- Understand the foundations of manifestation regarding biblical laws
- Integrate key biblical principles into your manifestation practice
- Leverage brain science to enhance your ability to manifest your desires
- Demystify manifestation because God created it, not man
- Align your thoughts with God's Word through meditation and prayer
- Overcome doubts and negative thoughts that hinder your progress
- Uncover roadblocks to manifesting an abundant, joyful life
- Develop a consistent manifestation routine that fits your lifestyle
- Sustain your manifestation success through long-term strategies

Interactive and Practical

This book is designed to be both interactive and practical. Each chapter features questions and exercises that prompt you to apply your newfound knowledge and assess your progress. These activities are designed to enrich your relationship with God by deepening your understanding of biblical truths while helping you internalize the principles and practices explored. By actively engaging with the material, you'll discover that your capacity to manifest your desires grows stronger and more dependable. You will also understand how our brains work and can help or block us from living a blessed life, and provide tools to clear the mess to discover the Masterpiece you were always intended to be.

A Journey of Faith and Transformation

Embarking on the manifestation journey is a multifaceted endeavor encompassing mental, spiritual, and emotional growth. It demands faith, commitment, and a willingness to evolve to transform your life and embrace the Masterpiece you were always created to be. As you navigate through this book, remember that you are not journeying alone; God's presence accompanies you, offering support at every turn if you seek and embrace it. Trust in His plan, remain dedicated to your practices, and keep your heart and mind open to the countless possibilities that await you. Additionally, consider joining my Facebook group, "Manifest God's Way," where you can ask questions and gain insights within a supportive community: (https://www.facebook.com/groups/450728911140075/permalink/4512472 87754904/)

My Story

When I was around eight years old, I found myself grappling with the complexities of life, questioning why—if God was as loving and good as people claimed, He would simply take me to heaven to be with Him. This period was marked by many significant events, both before and after that age, which I will share throughout this book to provide context for my struggles. At such a young age, I was enveloped in darkness, filled with confusion as I searched for answers. If the teachings of the Bible were indeed true, how could God allow me to endure the life I was living? Perhaps some of you can relate to that profound sense of bewilderment.

I vividly recall my great-grandmother moving away. She was the only source of genuine love that connected me to God and was family at the time. One night, as I lay in bed feeling utterly alone, I cried out to God, asking why He wouldn't just take me to heaven if He truly loved me. What transpired next became a moment etched in my memory and seared in my soul. It wasn't an audible voice but rather an inner knowing. I felt God reassuring me, saying, "I love you. You are my child, and I have good plans for you." One might assume that this revelation transformed my life into a sleepless, blissful journey filled with abundance and joy. However, that was just the beginning of my personal connection with really seeking God.

I also battled with my understanding of Him, influenced by my experiences within the church. At a young age, I often felt confused and even found myself at the altar confessing sins at just six years old, gripped by the fear of hell. It seemed unfathomable for a child to carry such burdens. The church I attended preached fire, brimstone, and damnation, instilling a fear of God within me until that beautiful moment of clarity. What could a six-year-old possibly need to confess? Yet, amidst the fear, there were also loving families around me that embodied the warmth of a Godly home, making me wonder if there was something better out there.

While I could share many details about the abusive environment I grew up in, the focus of this book is not to dwell on the past, which is beyond our control, but to rise above it and become the person God has always intended us to be. If you are currently facing a traumatic situation or experiencing abuse, please know that there is more help available today than ever before. Do not hesitate to reach out—abuse is never acceptable. I also recognize why the church became such a haven for a child like me: the church gave at least a semblance of something better, closer to what my soul felt was truth.

It's essential to recognize that while God established laws for our benefit, these same laws can be misused for harm, which was never His intention.

Let's Begin the Transformation

Are you prepared to change your life and bring your deepest desires to fruition? Let's embark on this transformative journey together, blending biblical wisdom, brain science, and authentic stories to cultivate a life filled with abundance, joy, and fulfillment. Open your heart, engage your mind, and allow the process of manifestation to unfold in alignment with God's divine purpose for you.

Welcome to a path that intertwines faith and science, showcasing the incredible blessings God has in store for you. Welcome to your new beginning! Welcome to discovering the Masterpiece you were always created to be! As you dive into this book, you will find more free resources on my site **https://msha.ke/warriorheartxo#links-2**

CHAPTER 1

The Foundations of Manifestation

Definition and Principles of Manifestation

Manifestation is a concept that has often been misunderstood, especially among those who have grown up in Christian communities and the broader spiritual realm. I have personally grappled with this topic, mainly as it gained traction in society and on social media, where it frequently became associated with greed and materialism. Even though I first encountered the idea of manifestation as a young girl, the fear of judgment from others made me hesitant to discuss it openly. This apprehension ultimately held me back from sharing my insights on a larger platform.

I have always been cautious about misrepresenting God or the teachings of the Bible. It's intriguing how a single word can become so fraught with misunderstanding that many people shy away from using it altogether—something I can relate to in my own journey. Years ago, I felt a strong calling to write and speak about manifestation in relation to God's biblical principles. Still, I held back due to fears of backlash, misunderstanding, or leading others astray. Recently, God has renewed my spirit, reminding me that the time has come to move forward and clear away those fears.

Throughout my over thirty years of experience, I have had the privilege of helping thousands of individuals break through their own barriers in various aspects of their lives through counseling and coaching. While I teach these principles, I, too, faced my own challenges with blocks from time to time. These obstacles can often be unconscious, a topic we will delve into further as we progress in this book.

Manifestation is fundamentally about transforming your thoughts, desires, and goals into reality through focused action and belief. It's rooted in the understanding that our thoughts, emotions, and actions are potent forces that shape our lives. Importantly, God's Word emphasizes that specific laws require both action and belief to manifest our desires, which are grounded in biblical teachings that we will explore in greater detail later on. God's Word also tells us in John 4:12, "Very truly I tell you, whoever believes in me will do the work I have been doing, and they will do even greater things than these, because I am going to the Father." Jesus was clear that we would be able to not only do what he did but also greater works.

I also believe that when we try to do things in our own power and understanding that we miss the opportunity of inviting God's wisdom and guidance, and much like the Israelites in the book of Deuteronomy and Numbers, a two-week journey could turn into a forty-year journey to get to the promised land. If you get stuck focusing on what you don't have already or that it's taking too long so you try something different—it's like planting a walnut tree and because you see no fruit you begin questioning God as if you did the wrong thing or you move away from your goal and it takes longer to come to past, but if you trust in the harvest and continue to go about toiling and tending to the other blessings and ideas God has given you, not only will that become a harvest eventually, but God will provide incredible blessings along the way just as He did for the Israelites giving them water, mana, and birds. He won't leave you in the desert without provisions. Even now as you read this book, I encourage you to get into a place in space where you ask God, "If I was in my most trusting place, what would I do right now to move more towards the blessings that you have in store for me?" Let Him guide your heart, mind, and soul. He loves you and wants good for you. Psalms 84:11 (ESV) declares, "For the Lord God is a sun and shield; the Lord Beto's favor and honor. No good thing does he withhold for those who walk uprightly." As we dive deeper, imagine your life with God guiding you in such love, peace, and joy as you let Him show you His way.

The principles of manifestation center around several key concepts: universal laws, intention, focus, belief, emotions, and action.

1. **Laws** are universal in nature, transcending race or social class. They serve as frameworks or procedures that offer guidance and direction. The Bible clearly presents these laws, and we will explore them in greater detail as we proceed.

2. **Intention** serves as the foundation for manifestation. It requires you to clearly articulate what you wish to achieve or invite into your life. When we know what we don't want, that is still professing what we want. When we pray specifically for what we want, it is like a fervent prayer. Without a defined intention, you may find yourself drifting through life, responding to circumstances, situations, people, and even the monkey mind without aiming for a specific outcome. I will dive deeper into this along the way. God illustrated this concept to me by comparing it to a leaf carried by the wind; without intention, you move aimlessly, swayed by external forces. It's akin to navigating through life without a map or GPS to guide you.

3. **Focus** involves directing your thoughts and emotions toward your desired outcome. This is where tools and techniques such as visualization and affirmations become essential. Scripture quotes can also serve as powerful affirmations. By consistently concentrating on what you wish to achieve, you can cultivate an emotional state that aligns harmoniously with your goals.

4. **Belief** is one of the most critical components of manifestation. It's essential to genuinely trust that your desires are attainable and that you have the capability to achieve them. You can enhance this belief by surrounding yourself with supportive individuals, engaging with positive content, and consistently nurturing your faith in the process.

5. **Emotions** are powerful feelings that can generate chemical reactions in both the body and the brain. They play a vital role in the manifestation process, yet they are often misunderstood. Understanding the impact of emotions is crucial for harnessing their potential effectively.

6. **Action** is the essential final piece of the puzzle. Although thoughts and beliefs hold significant power, they must be paired with concrete actions that propel you toward your goals. As God's Word states, "Faith without works is dead," highlighting the importance of taking realistic steps, working diligently, and maintaining persistence even when challenges arise. Ask God to give you one step you could take today to move closer to your blessings and prayers.

Manifestation goes beyond simple wishful thinking; it is a proactive approach that harmonizes mental, emotional, spiritual, and physical elements. This multifaceted process draws from various historical perspectives, emphasizing the importance of actively engaging in all aspects of life to bring your desires to fruition.

Historical Perspectives on Manifestation

The idea of manifestation has roots in diverse cultures and philosophies throughout history. From ancient civilizations to spiritual traditions and modern psychological theories, various insights reveal how humans have sought to harness the power of their minds to influence their realities. The field of psychology has significantly advanced our understanding of this concept, shedding light on the brain's workings and how our beliefs shape our behaviors and experiences.

In Christian history, manifestation has played a compelling role, encouraging believers to seek divine intervention and witness the transformative power of faith. Grounded in the teachings of Jesus Christ, manifestation emphasizes the belief that through prayer and aligning one's desires with God's Will, remarkable changes can occur. Stories of answered prayers, miraculous healings, and supernatural interventions have inspired believers for centuries, captivating their hearts and minds. Through practices like fasting and meditation, Christians have humbled themselves before God, opening up to divine guidance and revelations. Today, many continue to embrace manifestation, eagerly anticipating God's love and blessings in their lives. This rich aspect of Christian history reminds us of the profound impact faith can have when combined with a genuine desire to align with the Divine.

However, many Christians or individuals raised in Christian teachings face the challenge of reconciling these practices with their presence in other religions and cultures. It is essential to recognize that the laws governing manifestation are universal and can be applied in various ways. People from all walks of life have achieved success, prosperity, and healing by utilizing principles found in the Bible, even if they do not identify as Christian. This book will explore how the Bible illustrates these laws as pathways to an abundant and joyful life, acknowledging that trials and hardships are a part of the human experience. As the Bible states, "It rains on the just and the unjust," reminding us that all can face challenges, regardless of belief.

We will also delve into the psychology behind how our brain's wiring plays a crucial role in manifestation. Modern psychology links this concept to the theory of the "self-fulfilling prophecy," suggesting that our beliefs and expectations can shape our behaviors and the outcomes we encounter. Cognitive Behavioral Therapy (CBT) investigates the connections between thoughts, emotions, and actions, emphasizing how mental processes influence our lives. Many are familiar with the term self-sabotage, which describes the tendency to undermine our own efforts due to underlying belief systems. In upcoming chapters, we will explore this further. Psychology and counseling provide tools for individuals to examine and heal from harmful teachings or experiences that hinder healthy living. Visualization techniques have long been used in both sports and psychology and have also become the cornerstone in the emerging field of Spiritual Psychology. This field, which has gained recognition in recent years, offers fresh new insights into this fascinating journey of manifestation.

Introduction to Biblical Laws Related to Manifestation

The teachings in the Bible present a wealth of insights that resonate deeply with the principles of manifestation. These sacred scriptures lay a spiritual foundation for understanding how faith and belief can profoundly impact our lives.

One of the most powerful verses related to manifestation is found in Mark 11:24, which states, "Therefore I tell you, whatever you ask for in prayer, believe that you have received it, and it will be yours." This scripture beautifully encapsulates the essence of manifestation, highlighting the vital role of asking with unwavering faith.

Another significant passage is Matthew 17:20, where Jesus declares, "Truly I tell you, if you have faith as small as a mustard seed, you can say to this mountain, 'Move from here to there,' and it will move. Nothing will be impossible for you." This verse underscores the transformative potential of even the tiniest amount of faith and belief.

Proverbs 23:7 further illuminates the principle of manifestation with the phrase, "For as he thinks in his heart, so is he." This wisdom emphasizes the vital connection between our thoughts and our reality, suggesting that everything we internalize mentally and emotionally shapes our very existence.

The narrative of Abraham and Sarah in Genesis 15-21 is a powerful testament to manifestation through faith. Despite their advanced age and Sarah's initial barrenness, God's promise to Abraham—that he would become the father of many nations—was fulfilled because of their steadfast faith. This story illustrates the profound importance of trusting God's promises and believing in what may seem impossible.

Philippians 4:8 encourages believers to focus on uplifting and virtuous thoughts: "Finally, brothers and sisters, whatever is true, whatever is noble, whatever is right, whatever is pure, whatever is lovely, whatever is admirable— if anything is excellent or praiseworthy—think about such things." This scripture aligns beautifully with the principle of focus in manifestation, urging individuals to direct their thoughts toward positivity and inspiration.

Romans 12:2 speaks to the necessity of renewing one's mind: "Do not conform to the pattern of this world, but be transformed by the renewing of your mind. Then you will be able to test and approve what God's Will is—His good, pleasing, and perfect will." This verse highlights the significance of mental transformation and alignment with God's Will in the manifestation journey.

By understanding and applying these biblical principles, believers can tap into the immense power of faith and thought, manifesting the changes they desire in their lives. The Bible serves as a profound source of wisdom and guidance for anyone seeking to realize their goals and dreams in harmony with God's divine Will.

Conclusion

The principles of manifestation are intricately woven into both historical biblical teachings and the field of psychology. By intertwining the biblical laws, intention, focus, belief, and action, individuals can harness the transformative power of their thoughts and emotions to reshape their lives. The Bible provides profound wisdom on how faith and belief can significantly impact the outcomes we encounter. As we explore the dynamic relationship between biblical teachings and neuroscience in the upcoming chapters, we will reveal practical strategies for manifesting in alignment with God's Will, paving the way for a transformative journey that reflects His divine purpose in our lives.

Reflection Notes

CHAPTER 2

Biblical Principles of Manifestation

My Story

Why do I believe the Bible is so impactful? When I was about twelve, my neighbors, whom I had always gone to church with, had changed churches. I started going with them, and one day, my school bus driver, who attended the church we used to go to, told me I was going to hell for attending that kind of church, and so were all the people going there. I was just a kid, so I really struggled with this. I decided to stop going to church because I had some nightmares about judgment and hell. I decided to read the Bible myself. It was the best thing that ever happened to me because I began to see God's Word as a personal love story to everyone. I began to feel more drawn to a feeling, even then, that people were misinterpreting God's Word. It helped me clear a lot of things up and brought me closer to God. That's also around the time God gave me a calling to be a counselor and do missionary work. It was at this time that God showed me a lot about the differences between God's Word and man's interpretation. It was also a time for me to contemplate how I fit in the world and didn't.

Key Bible Scriptures Supporting Manifestation

The Bible is rich with verses highlighting the significance of faith, belief, and positive thinking, all of which are essential components of the manifestation concept. In this chapter, we will delve into several pivotal scriptures from the Bible, mainly from the New International Version (NIV) and King James Version (KJV), that bolster the idea of manifestation and explore how these teachings can be integrated into our everyday lives. I invite you to delve deeper as well. After each verse, write your thoughts about the meaning you make of each scripture below.

Mark 11:24 states, "Therefore I tell you, whatever you ask for in prayer, believe that you have received it, and it will be yours."

_____

_____

Matthew 17:20 further emphasizes, "He replied, 'Because you have so little faith. Truly I tell you, if you have faith as small as a mustard seed, you can say to this mountain, 'Move from here to there,' and it will move. Nothing will be impossible for you.'"

_____

_____

Proverbs 23:7 reminds us, "For as he thinks in his heart, so is he."

_____

_____

Philippians 4:8 encourages us with, "Finally, brothers and sisters, whatever is true, whatever is noble, whatever is right, whatever is pure, whatever is lovely, whatever is admirable—if anything is excellent or praiseworthy—think about such things."

_____

_____

Romans 12:2 advises, "Do not conform to the pattern of this world, but be transformed by the renewing of your mind. Then you will be able to test and approve what God's Will is—His good, pleasing, and perfect will."

_____

Hebrews 11:1 defines faith as "confidence in what we hope for and assurance about what we do not see."

Finally, John 14:13-14 assures us, "And I will do whatever you ask in my name, so that the Father may be glorified in the Son. You may ask me for anything in My name, and I will do it."

Exploring the Application of These Scriptures in Daily Life

The scriptures above provide a strong foundation for grasping the biblical principles of manifestation. By examining their meanings and practical applications, we can better understand how they guide us in harmonizing our thoughts, beliefs, and actions with God's Will. Let us explore their implications further.

Mark 11:24 underscores the necessity of belief in our prayers. It suggests that when we pray with genuine faith, we should embody the conviction that our prayers have already been answered. This scripture inspires us to maintain a positive outlook and unwavering faith in God's capacity to meet our needs and desires. It encourages us to adopt a hopeful and confident demeanor, trusting that what we seek through prayer is already on its way.

Viktor Frankl, in his profound work *Man's Search for Meaning*, illustrates how he utilized this belief to sustain his will to live while enduring the horrors of a concentration camp. He envisioned the meager food provided to him as something sumptuous and nourishing, imagining himself dining as a king. His imagination became a lifeline during one of the darkest chapters of his life. Even though he had people killed right beside him and he was given rotten food, he never wavered in his imaginative faith.

Matthew 17:20 teaches us that even the tiniest amount of faith can yield monumental changes. This verse is a powerful reminder that faith can indeed move mountains, symbolizing the ability to conquer seemingly insurmountable challenges. In our daily lives, this scripture encourages us to cultivate resilience and a steadfast mindset, assuring us that our faith can propel us toward our aspirations.

I have discovered a tool through God's Word that assisted me and enabled me to assist others. Matthew in the Bible recounts a father who sought healing for his son, prompting Jesus to affirm that all things are possible. The father, acknowledging his mustard seed-sized belief, implored, "Help my unbelief." I often visualize my faith as a tiny mustard seed, a mere speck at the tip of my pinky fingernail. I point this out to God, asking for help with the greater unbelief that resides within me. I wholeheartedly believe this scripture illustrates the miraculous healing of the man's son.

Proverbs 23:7 emphasizes the profound link between our thoughts and our reality. It suggests that our inner thoughts shape our identities and destinies. This verse stresses the importance of fostering positive and constructive thoughts. In our daily lives, we must remain vigilant about our internal dialogue, consciously replacing negative thoughts with affirmations that align with our aspirations.

One of my favorite books from my teenage years is *The Power of Positive Thinking* by Norman Vincent Peale. This influential work enlightened me about the profound impact of thoughts on our lives. God guided me to this book during my formative years to deepen my understanding of manifestation. Peale, a devout believer, provided valuable insights through various writings and guideposts that draw us closer to God and clarify the blessings that await us.

Philippians 4:8 encourages a focus on virtues that are true, noble, right, pure, lovely, and admirable. By directing our thoughts towards these qualities, we cultivate a mindset that attracts positive outcomes. We can apply this scripture by engaging in uplifting activities, consuming inspiring content, and surrounding ourselves with positive influences.

While some may dismiss the significance of what we watch or whom we associate with, both scripture and scientific research suggest otherwise. We will delve deeper into this topic later in the chapter.

Romans 12:2 speaks of the transformative power of renewing our minds. It encourages us to reject the negative patterns of the world and pursue a deeper understanding of God's Will. Practically, this involves a lifelong commitment to learning, growing, and aligning our thoughts with spiritual truths, facilitating a life that resonates with God's Plan for us.

Many individuals explore self-help literature or attend church services seeking change, but may fail to implement the necessary actions to cultivate a transformative lifestyle. Personally, I limit my television consumption and do not engage with the news unless absolutely necessary. Instead, I focus on areas I feel led to explore. In my upcoming book, where I write with a few other authors, I will shed deep scientific light into this area through the book *"Mindset Mastery: Unfunk Your Thinking, Rewire Your Brain and Unlock Your Full Potential,"* published in September 2025. You may also enjoy my TV show *The Masterpiece You Are,"* where I interview thought leaders in various fields on FENIX TV at https://fenixtv.app/

Hebrews 11:1 defines faith as the assurance of things hoped for and the conviction of things not seen. This scripture encourages a steadfast belief in the unseen and trust that our hopes will manifest. Practically, it invites us to maintain an optimistic outlook, even amidst challenging circumstances, and to act with confidence, believing that our faith will align with God's Desires for our lives.

Some may find it challenging to embrace this concept, fearing they are being dishonest if they do not acknowledge their current reality. However, research supports the notion that our thoughts can significantly influence our health and well-being. This understanding transcends mere wishful thinking; it is grounded in scientific evidence.

John 14:13-14 highlights the strength found in asking in Jesus' name. It reassures us that our prayers will be answered when our requests align with God's Will and are made with faith. We can incorporate this scripture into our daily lives by making prayer a routine, seeking divine guidance, and expressing gratitude for the blessings we receive, reinforcing our trust in the power of prayer.

Reflecting on Jesus, I see Him as an integral part of God. He teaches that He is one with the Father. It is essential to remember that the Bible, while written by human hands, is intended to guide us, not confuse us. If you find yourself struggling with any aspect of scripture, I encourage you to turn to God for clarity. Much of the Bible employs metaphorical language, reflecting its time's cultural and legal constraints. God guided the authors to convey wisdom in a manner that requires a personal connection with Him for deeper understanding.

When discussing God's nature, it is essential to recognize the use of pronouns like "he" and "him." While we are made in God's image, this refers to the spirit rather than physical attributes. The purpose of this book is not to delve into theological debates but to clarify that I will use these terms while acknowledging that God transcends gender and embodies both masculine and feminine energies. God is Spirit.

Let's look at the Bible in Real-Life Examples of Which Manifestation Is Played Out

The Bible is rich with narratives that exemplify the principles of manifestation through faith and belief. These accounts serve as powerful testimonies, showcasing how biblical teachings can profoundly transform lives.

The Journey of Abraham and Sarah: In Genesis 15-21, we encounter the profound journey of Abraham and Sarah. Despite their advanced age and Sarah's initial inability to conceive, God assured Abraham that he would become the father of a multitude of nations. Abraham's steadfast faith in God's promise culminated in the miraculous birth of Isaac. This story beautifully illustrates the significance of believing in God's assurances and highlights the virtues of patience and persistence in the manifestation process.

Think about modern-day stories you've been told that replicate this miracle. I honestly can tell you of countless people I have met over the years who fit similar profound magical moments that looked bleak, but God... showed up and changed everything.

I remember a particular individual who came to work with me after losing a baby. She had been told that it would be difficult to conceive. Doctors had even given evidence of science with tests that confirmed it would be difficult. But what she heard was that it could be impossible to conceive. When she came, we first worked on letting her grieve the child she lost; otherwise, the unprocessed feelings would leave a block to her faith in the miracle she received a few months later and held healthy, whole, and flourishing nine months after that with a wonderful, positive pregnancy. I also worked with her husband to process and heal, plus rewire for a positive, healthy pregnancy and birth. I love to let God guide me through these beautiful moments as we create together a healing place for them to rewire and change the legacy of their lives and their families. I love these reports. Not only does she and her spouse get to celebrate, but also everyone around her begins to believe once again in miracles.

Think about a miracle(s) you recall:

_____

_____

_____

_____

The Life of Joseph: The Saga of Joseph, narrated in Genesis 37-50, stands as a remarkable testament to manifestation through unwavering faith and resilience.

After being sold into slavery by his own brothers and enduring countless hardships, Joseph never wavered in his belief in God's divine plan. His optimistic outlook and steadfast faith ultimately elevated him to become the second most powerful figure in Egypt. Joseph's story teaches us the importance of maintaining integrity and faith, even amidst adversity.

What modern-day story comes to mind for you? For me, there are several where people I know had difficulties in a career, and though everything in them wanted to give up, they stayed praying through and living in integrity and, in the end, were elevated in different ways or vindicated.

Reflect on a story you know that has these similarities:

_____

_____

_____

_____

The Healing of the Woman with the Issue of Blood: In Mark 5:25-34, we learn about a woman who had suffered from a bleeding condition for twelve long years. She believed that merely touching Jesus' cloak would restore her health. Her faith was so profound that upon making contact with his garment, she was instantly healed. Jesus recognized her faith, declaring, "Daughter, your faith has healed you. Go in peace and be freed from your suffering." This narrative underscores the transformative power of faith and the belief that God can deliver miraculous solutions to our challenges.

I, too, know many people who have been healed over the years. Some were in an instance, and some had the issue for years before miraculously healing. I, too, have pondered this. I have found it best not to delve too deep into WHYs of life and will explain more in upcoming chapters. I have embraced the belief that it could be today. Yes, what if today is the day… I began to say, "I allow, I accept, I receive the blessing you have for me, Lord." My thoughts now drift from "why" to "is there anything in my way keeping me from making it so," and if so, I release and let it go.

Is there a miracle you can recall where it had long been a problem, but then instantly changed?

_____

_____

_____

_____

The Encounter Between David and Goliath: In 1 Samuel 17, we witness the young shepherd David confront the formidable giant, Goliath, armed only with a sling and a few stones. Despite the overwhelming odds, David's faith in God's power remained unshakable. His confidence and trust in divine intervention enabled him to conquer Goliath and protect the Israelites. This story exemplifies the vital role of faith and courage in overcoming obstacles and achieving remarkable victories.

What Giants have you or those you know slain?

_____

_____

_____

_____

The Story of Hannah: In 1 Samuel 1, we meet Hannah, a woman who longed for a child. She prayed earnestly to God, vowing that if He granted her a son, she would dedicate him to His service. God answered her heartfelt prayers, and she gave birth to Samuel, who would rise to become a great prophet. Hannah's journey is a testament to the power of persistent prayer and the fulfillment of God's promises.

The Faith of Daniel: The book of Daniel reveals how Daniel's unwavering faith and trust in God allowed him to flourish even in captivity. His steadfast belief in God's protection enabled him to survive the lion's den unscathed. Daniel's story illustrates the power of persistent faith and the assurance that God will deliver and safeguard those who place their trust in Him.

Do you recall a time when someone you knew was protected and saved from perils?

_____

_____

_____

The Tale of Shadrach, Meshach, and Abednego: In the Book of Daniel, it exemplifies unwavering faith and courage in the face of persecution. When King Nebuchadnezzar demanded that they worship a golden idol, the three young men boldly refused, declaring their loyalty to the God of Israel despite the threat of a fiery furnace. Miraculously, they emerged from the flames unscathed, accompanied by a divine presence that astonished the king. This powerful narrative underscores the importance of standing firm in one's beliefs. It illustrates that true strength comes from faith, serving as a timeless reminder that unwavering trust in God can lead to miraculous deliverance and inspire others to recognize the power of faith.

Whether you look at the story of Joseph being abandoned by his own family, Daniel in the lion's den, or Shadrach, Meshach, and Abednego thrown into the fires to be consumed... May I bid you to see that the miracles within these stories are still alive today. The God of their soul is still the God who longs to answer your deepest, desperate prayers.

One of my favorite modern-day historical events has to do with the life of Nelson Mandela. Nelson Mandela, a pillar of hope and resilience, faced imprisonment from the very society he sought to uplift. Initially viewed with skepticism within his own community, Mandela's unwavering commitment to his spiritual beliefs and values ultimately transformed him into a beacon of unity. Mandela was raised in a Christian home. Even during his 27 years behind bars, he clung to the principles of forgiveness, justice, and equality, which fortified his spirit and inspired countless others. Upon his release, Mandela emerged not merely as a freed man but as a leader whose faith in humanity transcended the barriers of division, guiding South Africa toward reconciliation and healing. His journey from prisoner to president serves as a powerful testament to the strength of belief and the enduring human spirit.

Could you weather these storms? Oh, but maybe you already have! Have you forgotten? Maybe this is your call to remember. This book is designed to help you dive deep into your journey, so let's take a moment for deeper reflection.

Let's Dive Deeper:

1. Engage in a Meaningful Reflection on Your Beliefs

What core beliefs shape your understanding of the world and God or a Higher Power?

_____

_____

_____

_____

Do you view the Bible as a guide that enhances your spiritual connection and deepens your comprehension of life through faith?

_____

_____

_____

_____

Can you identify specific instances where you applied biblical principles in your prayers and felt a response from God?

_____

_____

_____

_____

What lessons can you draw from your spiritual journey that might help you overcome obstacles you face today?

_____

_____

_____

_____

Reflect on a time when your faith was tested—how did that experience shape your beliefs moving forward?

_____

_____

_____

_____

2. Scripture Affirmations

Which of the scriptures above resonate with you?

_____

_____

_____

_____

Write down some of your favorite scriptures dealing with faith and belief.

_____

_____

_____

_____

3. Visualize Using Scriptures

Visualize times in your life when God answered those prayers. Remember to tap into what it felt like when you asked for the prayer, especially when He answered it. Reflect on the practice.

_____

_____

_____

_____

4. Prayer and Meditation Practice

The teachings of the Word of God emphasize the importance of dedicating time to both prayer and meditation. In my view, prayer is the act of reaching out to God to express our desires and needs. Meditation, on the other hand, involves reflecting on the scriptures and contemplating what they reveal about specific aspects of our lives and prayers, allowing us to sit in stillness and be receptive to God's guidance. It is essential to carve out time for a practice that intertwines engaging with God's Word in relation to your prayers while embracing moments of stillness to listen for His direction. This sacred space fosters a deeper connection, enabling us to align our hearts with His Will. Reflect on your practice.

_____

_____

_____

_____

5. Praises

At the beginning or end of each day, take a moment to jot down the ways in which God has answered your prayers. Expressing gratitude for our blessings is a clear directive from God, and this practice serves as a powerful tool in our spiritual journey. I cherish this habit as it helps me recognize the countless times God has responded to my prayers and intentions and the abundant blessings present in my life. By reflecting on these moments, we cultivate a heart of thankfulness and deepen our appreciation for His grace and provision. This is particularly valuable during challenging times, as it reminds us of the moments when He has answered our prayers. Reflect on your practice.

_____

_____

_____

_____

Exercise

For one week, try this practice. Get a journal and, first thing in the morning or in the evening, acknowledge and write down all of the blessings, miracles, or answered prayers that happened. In the morning or evening, think on these things you have written, with great gratitude in your heart, body, and mind, and feel these blessings. After that week, notice the difference in how you feel daily. You can experiment by shifting which time you write them out and which time you just replay them and relish in their bliss. Continue this practice or one similar for as long as you wish, and blessings will flow to you more easily.

Conclusion

The biblical principles of manifestation are profoundly anchored in faith, belief, and a positive mindset. Scripture offers us clear guidance on how to align our thoughts, beliefs, and actions with God's Will to bring our desires into reality. By understanding and applying these principles in our everyday lives, we can tap into the power of faith, fostering positive transformations and reaching our God-given potential. Real-life examples from the Bible and current events further illustrate the transformative impact of our beliefs and our trust in God's promises. As we delve deeper into the relationship between biblical teachings and brain science in the upcoming chapters, we will uncover practical strategies for manifesting in accordance with God's Will and living a life that resonates with His divine plan. As you daily commit to your first rewiring exercise for abundance by tapping into the power of gratitude, which will be covered more later in depth.

Reflection Notes

CHAPTER 3

The Science of the Brain

Basic Understanding of Brain Functions Related to Thoughts

The human brain is an incredibly intricate and sophisticated organ that governs our thoughts, beliefs, emotions, and actions. With a background in counseling psychology, I have dedicated my life to understanding and helping others explore the neuropsychology of the brain, which plays a crucial role in enhancing our lives. Recognizing the brain's essential functions reveals how our thoughts and beliefs shape our reality. It's vital to remember that the brain is an organ, and understanding its workings is necessary for effecting meaningful change in our lives. I often remind people to think of it like this... The brain and the heart are just organs with stored memories and connections; it is our soul that leaves the body when we die. In order to truly change our lives, we must look at the brain and body as a programming system that requires us to rewire the parts that have errors. Much like a computer or phone, you have to regularly find the system errors and download new software. I believe knowledge is power, so when I work with individuals, this is one of the first things I teach them, so they can better understand and utilize their brain's systems. I could write a whole book on this, as many have already, but I want to at least get you thinking about how your brain and body work in order to dive deeper and clear your mess to discover your Masterpiece.

The brain is composed of various regions, each responsible for different functions. The cerebral cortex, the brain's outer layer, is divided into four lobes: frontal, parietal, temporal, and occipital. The frontal lobe is key for decision-making, problem-solving, and regulating behavior and emotions, while the temporal lobe plays a critical role in memory and language comprehension. The occipital lobe is primarily responsible for vision. Although the brain has many components, we will focus on a few key areas for simplicity. As more people explore the connection between the brain and body, it's important to note that neurons are also found throughout the body, influencing various aspects of our lives. Among these neurons is a cluster located in the brainstem known as the reticular activating system, which we will discuss further.

Understanding our thought and belief systems involves key structures such as the hippocampus, amygdala, and hypothalamus. The limbic system is deeply engaged in emotional regulation, memory formation, and processing rewards and punishments. This highlights the importance of studying the brain in relation to our belief systems and the influences of our upbringing, as these factors can significantly impact our faith outcomes as well as our intentions.

Neurons, the brain's fundamental building blocks, communicate through electrical impulses and chemical signals. When neurons in specific areas of the brain activate, they form neural networks that strengthen over time through a process called neuroplasticity—the brain's remarkable ability to rewire itself by creating new connections. This capacity enables us to learn new things, develop new habits, and alter our thought patterns. Isn't it fascinating that our understanding of the brain's malleability has only emerged over the past 30 years?

Beliefs are essentially thoughts we accept as true, formed through repeated experiences and reinforced by our environment and social interactions. Many of our beliefs are shaped during childhood. When we hold a belief, the related neural pathways in the brain become more pronounced, making it easier to think in ways that align with that belief. It's intriguing to realize that from before birth until around age seven, we are continuously programmed by our surroundings. Our parents, television, community, family, school, church, siblings, friends, and daycares all contribute to the wiring of our brains. Remarkably, we begin hearing in utero around 18 weeks. Throughout my years of work, I have encountered individuals who recall traumatic experiences from this early stage, as well as many who have faced childhood traumas or even benign experiences that left lasting imprints in their brains. These experiences can create beliefs that persist throughout life. However, with the proper support, individuals can work through these issues, rewiring their thought patterns and clearing away the emotional weight they carry. I recall a particular instance working with an individual on the triggered response he was having, and when we dove deep to clear it, he had an image in the womb as if he were dying. He felt such peace after clearing it, but also a discombobulating feeling of not knowing why. So, he asked his mother and found that his mother had been strangled during her pregnancy with him, and she never told him due to the circumstances around it. With the new information, he easily sinks into releasing it all.

Our brains are extraordinary; however, we often function in autopilot mode in our daily lives. It takes us looking at our lives with curiosity, examining areas we want to change more clearly, and then having the courage to break the programming. Plus, there may be programs that are truly unconscious to us, that take an even deeper dive using tools like EMDR, hypnosis, and such to find, process, and release. We truly are a Masterpiece!

"You Can NOT Change What You Do Not NOTICE"
—Erica Elliot

How the Brain Processes and Stores Information

The brain processes and stores information through a sophisticated system encompassing encoding, storage, and retrieval.

Encoding is the initial step in this information processing journey. It involves transforming sensory input into a format that can be stored within the body. This crucial process takes place in the hippocampus, a key structure in the limbic system that is essential for forming new memories. The significance and emotional resonance of information heavily influence how it is encoded; experiences that are particularly meaningful or emotionally charged are more likely to be etched deeply into our brains.

Storage refers to the maintenance of this encoded information over time. The brain categorizes memories into two primary types: short-term and long-term memory. Short-term memory, often called working memory, temporarily holds information for immediate use, but its capacity and duration are limited. In contrast, long-term memory boasts a much larger capacity and can retain information for extended periods, ranging from hours to a lifetime.

Long-term memory can be further divided into explicit (or declarative) memory and implicit (or nondeclarative) memory. Explicit memory encompasses facts and events we can consciously recall—such as names, dates, and personal experiences—while implicit memory involves skills and habits like riding a bike or playing a musical instrument that we perform without conscious awareness.

Retrieval is the process of accessing stored information when needed. The effectiveness of retrieval hinges on how well the information was encoded and stored. Retrieval cues—contextual or sensory stimuli linked to the original encoding—can enhance this process significantly. The prefrontal cortex plays a vital role in retrieval, helping us organize and access the information we need.

Memory is not a static process; it is dynamic and reconstructive. Each time we recall a memory, we may subtly alter it based on new experiences and information. This reconstructive nature of memory explains why recollections can shift over time and why two individuals may remember the same event in different ways.

Because we may have information stored that we may not even realize is stored the way it is unconsciously, there are so many tools that can help us to look at the information we may not have noticed before so that we can shift and change it for the better. We will explore more tools along the way, but for now, as my quote above states, "You can NOT change what you do not Notice." I implore you to begin to notice how these intricate parts work in your life.

The brain's capacity to process and store information can be significantly enhanced through various practices. Repetition and rehearsal strengthen neural connections, facilitating easier recall. Elaborative encoding, which involves linking new information to existing knowledge, can also boost memory retention. For instance, creating associations or using mnemonic devices can aid in remembering complex information more effectively.

Adopting healthy lifestyle choices is crucial for supporting optimal brain function. Regular physical exercise increases blood flow to the brain, promoting the growth of new neurons and enhancing cognitive abilities. A balanced diet rich in antioxidants, omega-3 fatty acids, and other essential nutrients helps protect the brain from oxidative stress and supports overall cognitive health.

Stress management is another vital aspect of maintaining brain health. Chronic stress can harm the hippocampus, impairing memory and cognitive function. Engaging in practices such as mindfulness meditation, deep breathing exercises, and spending time in nature can help mitigate stress and promote mental well-being.

Conclusion

Gaining a deeper understanding of the brain's science reveals how our thoughts and beliefs shape our reality. The brain's remarkable adaptability, fueled by neuroplasticity, empowers us to alter our thought patterns and cultivate new habits through positive thinking and visualization. By tapping into the brain's reward system and engaging in practices that foster mental and emotional well-being, we can significantly enhance our ability to manifest our desires.

The processes of encoding, storing, and retrieving information are fundamental to our learning and memory. By utilizing techniques that support these processes—such as repetition, elaborative encoding, and making healthy lifestyle choices—we can optimize our cognitive function and improve our capacity to achieve our goals.

As we delve into the connection between biblical principles and brain science in the upcoming chapters, we will uncover practical strategies for harnessing the power of our minds to create a life that aligns with God's Will. By integrating these insights into our daily routines, we can transform our thoughts and beliefs into tangible outcomes, enabling us to fulfill our God-given potential.

Identify Neural Pathways

Question: As you reflect on the paragraphs above, consider how your beliefs have been shaped throughout your life.

_____

_____

Exercise: Take a moment to write down your beliefs regarding the brain, manifestation, and the Bible. What do you believe about manifestation and how the Bible and brain contribute or don't?

_____

_____

_____

_____

Next, examine where these beliefs originated. Have they evolved over the years? If so, what prompted those changes?

_____

_____

_____

_____

Question: How does the concept of neuroplasticity illustrate the brain's capacity for change and adaptation?

_____

_____

Exercise: Write a brief paragraph describing a personal experience in which you learned a new skill or transformed a habit. Reflect on how repeated practice and focused effort helped you create new neural pathways and consider how this understanding can aid in developing positive thoughts and beliefs.

_____

_____

_____

_____

Neuroscience Behind Positive Thinking and Visualization

Positive thinking and visualization are potent tools that can significantly impact the brain's structure and function. Research in neuroscience offers compelling evidence that these practices can improve both mental and physical well-being, and it's exciting to see that the Word of God aligns with these findings.

Positive thinking entails directing our focus toward uplifting thoughts and emotions, which can lead to improved mood, reduced stress, and better overall health. The brain's reward system, particularly through neurotransmitters like dopamine and serotonin, plays a crucial role in this process. These chemicals are linked to feelings of happiness and pleasure. Engaging in positive thinking activates the brain's reward pathways, reinforcing affirmative thought patterns and making it easier to sustain a positive mindset.

Positive thinking and visualization have long been integral components of athletic training, helping athletes enhance their performance and overcome mental barriers. Over the years, many renowned athletes have embraced these techniques, demonstrating their effectiveness in achieving peak performance. By cultivating a positive mindset and vividly imagining successful outcomes, athletes can significantly improve their focus, resilience, and overall game strategy.

Visualization is the practice of crafting vivid mental images of desired outcomes. This technique taps into the brain's ability to simulate experiences and has been shown to enhance performance, alleviate anxiety, and boost motivation. Remarkably, the brain often struggles to distinguish between real and imagined experiences; when we visualize, we activate the same neural networks involved in actual experiences. One way you can test this is to close your eyes if you are in a safe, seated-down position and imagine going up on an elevator to the 45th floor as you step out the door onto the roof, walk to the edge and lean over the edge, seeing the ground below with cars below beeping and feeling the wind as it rocks you a bit. Pretty interesting, isn't it?

Research has shown that visualization can lead to tangible improvements in athletic performance. For instance, studies involving Olympic athletes have revealed that those who practiced mental imagery consistently experienced greater success compared to those who did not. Visualization allows athletes to mentally rehearse their movements, enabling them to refine their skills and prepare for competition. This mental practice engages the same neural pathways that are activated during physical performance, effectively reinforcing the muscle memory required for success.

Research indicates that athletes who employ visualization techniques can enhance their performance nearly as effectively as those who engage in physical practice. This occurs because visualization activates the motor cortex, responsible for planning and executing movements. Fascinating studies demonstrate that when individuals are connected to electrodes while performing an action, such as hitting a ball, and then tested visualizing the same action, the same areas of the brain and muscles light up. Isn't that incredible! Through consistent visualization of specific actions, individuals can strengthen the neural pathways associated with those actions, ultimately leading to improved performance.

Moreover, positive thinking plays a crucial role in an athlete's ability to cope with the pressures of competition. By maintaining an optimistic outlook, athletes can reduce anxiety and stress, leading to improved concentration and decision-making during high-stakes moments. Coaches and sports psychologists often emphasize the importance of fostering a positive mindset, encouraging athletes to replace self-doubt with affirmations of confidence and belief in their abilities.

As the field of sports psychology continues to evolve, the integration of positive thinking and visualization into training regimens has become more sophisticated. Athletes are now equipped with tools to harness the power of their minds, allowing them to push past limitations and achieve extraordinary feats. Through dedication to these mental techniques, many have found that success in sports is as much a mental game as it is a physical one, proving that the mind can be a powerful ally in the pursuit of excellence.

As a child, physical education was a staple for all of us, and many of us also participated in various sports. I dabbled in basketball, softball, baseball, volleyball, and even track. Through these experiences, I acquired valuable life skills such as teamwork, the importance of relentless practice, and the dedication required to improve. Although I was involved in numerous sports, I didn't fully grasp how powerful visualization techniques could be at that time. We learned the basics, like drawing diagrams and imagining passes or defensive moves, but I later discovered that these concepts could be applied on a much deeper level in athletics.

My understanding of visualization blossomed when I began reading books on the subject. During my time in the military, we utilized various neuro-connecting tools designed to help us remember procedures more effectively. These techniques made it easier to visualize tasks and execute them swiftly. It was during my college years, while playing tennis, that I truly harnessed the power of visualization. By actively imagining successful serves and strategic plays, I found that my performance improved significantly, reinforcing the idea that the mind and body work in tandem to achieve excellence.

One of my favorite movies that depicts using visualization is *Cool Runnings*, which tells the heartwarming story of the Jamaican bobsled team that made history by competing in the Winter Olympics. Despite coming from a country with no snow, the team, driven by their dreams and determination, embodied the power of visualization and positive thinking. They envisioned themselves as champions, overcoming numerous obstacles along the way. Their journey highlights the essence of teamwork and the belief that with passion and perseverance, one can manifest their dreams, regardless of the circumstances. The story serves as a reminder that success often begins in the mind and can be achieved through unwavering commitment and the support of a united team. If you've never seen the movie, I would highly recommend it.

Positive thinking and visualization are not only for sports enthusiasts. I have worked with thousands of people through the years, helping them with everything from performing on stage to presenting at work, interviewing, talking through a difficult conversation, driving, flying, and so much more. I myself have used these tools countless times for singing on stage, performing a speech or test anxiety, talking with someone over difficult situations, and so much more, with amazing success, and when I pray and ask God's guidance, even better.

Positive thinking and visualization also influence the prefrontal cortex, the area of the brain involved in planning, decision-making, and emotional regulation. By concentrating on positive outcomes and visualizing success, we can enhance activity in this region, leading to better emotional control and more effective problem-solving skills.

Mindfulness meditation, which combines elements of positive thinking and visualization—often through the lens of scripture—has demonstrated significant effects on brain structure and function. Regular mindfulness practice can increase gray matter density in the prefrontal cortex and hippocampus, areas associated with memory, learning, and emotional regulation. Additionally, it can reduce the size of the brain's fear center, promoting a greater sense of calm and resilience.

Now, I want to be clear, I am not advocating that we negate negatives in such a way that we create positive toxicity. Which I will explore more in the following chapters.

Interactive Questions and Exercises

1. Practicing Positive Thinking

Question: How do neurotransmitters like dopamine and serotonin affect your mood and intentions?

_____

_____

Exercise: Keep a "Positive Thinking Journal" for a week. Each day, write down three positive thoughts or affirmations. Note any changes in your mood, motivation, or overall well-being at the end of the week. Reflect on how positive thinking influences your brain chemistry.

_____

_____

_____

_____

2. Visualization Techniques

Question: What is the difference between detailed mental imagery and future self-visualization?

_____

_____

Exercise: Choose a specific goal you want to achieve. Spend 10 minutes each day visualizing the goal completed successfully using detailed mental imagery. Engage your senses to create a vivid picture. Write down your experiences and any insights gained from this practice in your journal. Reflect on the practice.

_____

_____

_____

_____

3. Creating Effective Visualizations

Question: How can you ensure your visualizations are as effective as possible? Write what you've learned.

_____

_____

Exercise: Create a visualization script, write a detailed description of your goal, including sensory details and emotions associated with achieving it. Write as if you have already obtained the goal with joy and excitement. Read the script aloud during your visualization. Practice creates changes with confidence and motivation over time.

_____

_____

_____

_____

CHAPTER 4

How the Brain Processes Information

A Process System That Involves Coding, Storage, and Retrieval

Have you ever stopped to think about how incredibly powerful your mind is—not just spiritually, but biologically? God didn't just design you to think and feel; He created a divine masterpiece in your brain that can learn, adapt, renew, and even heal itself over time. Every single thought you think, prayer you pray, or memory you hold doesn't simply vanish—it leaves an imprint. That imprint is real. It's biological. And it's spiritual.

The brain processes information through an intricate dance between neurons—nerve cells that transmit electrical impulses—and chemical messengers called **neurotransmitters**. When you focus your attention on something, your brain forms synaptic connections that begin to wire together. This is often summed up by the phrase: "neurons that fire together, wire together." Over time, repeated thoughts become automatic—like deeply worn trails in your mental landscape. This is why worry can feel habitual, and why faith, once practiced, can also become second nature.

This is what **neuroplasticity** is all about—the brain's God-given ability to change based on experience. Your brain is not fixed or stuck. It was designed by the Creator to renew, to grow, to shift. And guess what? That design aligns beautifully with Scripture. "Do not conform to the pattern of this world, but be transformed by the renewing of your mind" (Romans 12:2, NIV). That verse isn't just poetic encouragement—it's a divine blueprint for rewiring your brain.

Now, let's slow this down and go deeper. Your **short-term memory**, also called **working memory**, is like a mental whiteboard—temporary, active, and limited in capacity. It holds information for just a few seconds or minutes while your brain decides what to do with it. Unless that information is **rehearsed**, repeated, or tied to strong emotion, it won't be transferred to long-term memory. It gets wiped away.

The **hippocampus**, a seahorse-shaped structure deep in your brain, acts like a gateway, transferring information from short-term memory to long-term storage. But it doesn't make that decision on its own. It needs signals—either through repetition or emotion. If you repeat something consistently or experience something with intense emotional charge, your hippocampus marks it as important and files it away.

Here's the twist: emotionally negative events are stored faster and more vividly than positive ones. That's because your **amygdala**, the brain's emotional alarm system, tags painful or threatening events with a priority marker. This built-in **negativity bias** was designed to help you survive—to remember what hurt you so you could avoid it next time. But while this helps with survival, it often becomes a stronghold of fear and false identity.

That's why a harsh word, betrayal, or moment of shame from years ago can still come up instantly, while a kind word or encouraging moment might be forgotten by morning. Positive truths, including God's Word, don't always stick right away—not because they're not powerful, but because they require more conscious repetition to become rooted.

This is where the spiritual discipline of **renewing your mind** becomes practical, powerful, and even biological. When the Bible says, "Faith comes by hearing, and hearing by the word of God" (Romans 10:17, NKJV), it's revealing the brain's design: repetition forms retention. You must hear it again and again. Every time you rehearse God's truth—whether speaking it, meditating on it, or journaling it—you are sending signals to the hippocampus: "Store this. Anchor this. I want this to become part of me."

And the brain listens. Over time, those new truths form stronger neural connections. What was once unfamiliar begins to feel familiar. What once felt like a stretch becomes second nature. That's how healing happens. That's how trauma begins to loosen its grip. And that's how you begin to walk in the truth of your identity, not the residue of your past.

So, when you declare, "I am fearfully and wonderfully made" (Psalm 139:14), your brain doesn't just hear words—it receives instruction. If repeated often enough, with intention and belief, your brain will rewire to align with that truth. That's what scripture meant when it spoke of meditating day and night. It's not for God's benefit. It's for ours. Repetition is how **short-term truth becomes long-term transformation**.

Prayer and meditation, then, aren't passive spiritual habits. They are **active neurological tools**. Brain imaging studies now show that regular spiritual practices—like prayer, gratitude, and scripture meditation—thicken gray matter in the **prefrontal cortex** (the part of your brain that governs focus, compassion, and decision-making) and shrink overactivity in the amygdala (where fear is processed). Simply put: the more you dwell in God's presence and truth, the more peaceful, clear, and resilient your mind becomes.

This isn't wishful thinking. It's Heaven's blueprint meeting biological function. God designed the brain to renew—**with Him at the center**. Your thoughts can be transformed. Your emotions can be redirected. Your inner dialogue can begin to reflect His promises. But only if you **practice**. Not once. Not twice. **Daily. Repeatedly. Intentionally.**

What you rehearse, you will retrieve. What you retrieve, you will reinforce. And what you reinforce, you will believe. That belief becomes your new inner atmosphere—the space where God's breath fills every cell with life, peace, and direction.

God's ways are higher, but He didn't leave us powerless. He gave us a brain that can change, a Spirit that guides, and a Word that rewires. The breath of Heaven is not just poetic—it's physiological. Every time you speak life, dwell in truth, and turn your heart toward God, you are bringing Heaven into your biology and building the mind of Christ within your very own brain.

Interactive Questions and Exercises for Understanding Memory Processes

Question: What are the main differences between short-term and long-term memory?

_____

_____

Exercise: Create a memory for a topic you are passionate about. Start with the central idea branch, related concepts, and details. Use this map to practice encoding and retrieving information. Reflect on how this exercise strengthens your memory. This is a great way to see how you think about a topic.

_____

_____

_____

_____

Here Are a Few Examples of Memory Mapping:

Example 1:

Money

Currency, Coins

Credit Cards, Spending, Buying

Gifts, Receiving, Fun, Going Out to Eat, Vacation

I remember going out to eat and thinking how wonderful that I have money to do this. I didn't have those opportunities when I was a kid.

Let me also say I have worked hard to clear the mess in my mind for scarcity.

Let's track the next one with a scarcity mindset.

Example 2:

Money

Currency, Coins, Checks

Credit Cards, Loans, Debt

Spending, Buying, Need to Work Hard

Doesn't Grow on Trees, Hard to Come By, Gone Quickly, Never Enough

Do you see how the same word could have positive or negative thoughts associated with it?

The great thing is that with a little practice, you can open your mind, clear the mess, and rewire for greater success. You see, if your unconscious thoughts have a negative belief, you will have what psychology calls a negative bias towards it. I will review this more in a bit, but for now, let's do another.

Example 3:

Bible

God, Religion, Jesus

Church, Community, Rules

I loved going to church as a kid. It was a safe place for me, and I felt loved. I didn't understand why churches had so many disagreements with one another, which made me sad. As an adult, God is still love, but God, the Bible, and religion are not the same. We are the church, not a building, and many have been taught wrong about the meaning of things written in the Bible, using it like a whip, which makes me sad. My thoughts and concepts have changed since I was a kid.

I want to expand on negative and positive bias so you can get a better idea of why it's so important to review this in your life, so you reduce blocks to blessings. Whether you believe it or not, all of us have biases, and these biases come from sources like our family, schools, peers, religion, and society. Most people will never know this unless they go through a psychology course or some type of learning that delves into this, but I believe it's important to know, understand, and decipher this for yourself.

Bias factors, both negative and positive, significantly influence our learning experiences, particularly in the context of family, religion, education, culture, and relationships. Negative bias often manifests in familial settings where past conflicts or criticisms are remembered more vividly than positive interactions. For instance, a child raised in a critical environment may internalize negative feedback, leading to a mindset that prioritizes perceived failures over successes. This can create a cycle of self-doubt and anxiety that hinders personal growth and learning, as the individual may avoid new experiences for fear of criticism.

Conversely, positive bias factors can emerge from supportive family dynamics and religious teachings that emphasize love, acceptance, and understanding. In such environments, individuals may be more likely to embrace new learning opportunities and develop a sense of self-efficacy. Religious teachings that promote forgiveness and compassion can foster resilience, encouraging individuals to view challenges as opportunities for growth rather than threats. However, an overly positive bias may lead to unrealistic expectations, where individuals overlook necessary critiques or challenges within their relationships or beliefs.

Ultimately, the interplay of negative and positive biases shapes how individuals learn from their familial, school, society, or religious contexts. Recognizing these biases can help individuals navigate their lives more effectively, leading to healthier processing and deeper understanding. By fostering an awareness of both the positive and negative influences within their upbringing, individuals can work towards a more balanced perspective that enhances their learning and personal development. This is why it is crucial for you to review your thoughts and ideas around things you want in life. You may be unconsciously sabotaging yourself from creating a life you dream of having.

I used to have a mindset that only General Motors vehicles were worth having because most of my family told me so, and if I liked a foreign car, then I was being communist. I was also told never to buy an Apple phone because they manipulate you and take your information, and many other things. My husband bought me an Apple phone to go with my Apple iPad. It helps me a lot to get more done since they are connected. I also recall many of the thoughts from my church upbringing that money is evil or that rich people are prideful. I know lots of people who are wealthy who are so giving and loving today. You can see how something can get logged in the brain and create a problem in your life.

Now, you try. Write out all of the thoughts you have about money, God, yourself, and any other area in which you are associated with your big dreams. See if you notice any negative associations that need to be cleared.

_____

_____

_____

_____

_____

_____

_____

_____

_____

_____

_____

Enhancing Memory Through Repetition

Question: How does repetition help strengthen neural connections and improve memory retention?

_____

_____

Exercise: Choose a new skill or a piece of information you want to learn. Dedicate a few minutes each day to practice or review it. Note your progress over a month and write a reflection on how repetition has helped improve your mastery of the skill or information.

A prime example of learning through repetition that stands out in my memory is the mantra I often heard: "read, write, recite." This approach was particularly emphasized during my college years, but I believe it serves as an effective learning tool for students of all ages.

Exercise: Choose a few aspirations and write them as if you already have them three times in the morning, three times in the afternoon, and three times in the evening.

_____

_____

_____

_____

Examples:

I am grateful I am healed

I am so blessed, and more blessings are pouring into my life

I am so thankful for the people I get to help all around the world heal

I am grateful I have an amazing, healthy, supportive relationship

I am so grateful I am debt-free, and money pours into my life with ease

I am so thankful that I am a successful speaker, doctor, and entrepreneur

I am so grateful and appreciative of the upbeat clients who flow to me with ease and joy

I am so grateful that I stay focused and organized with ease

I am so appreciative and thankful for an amazing house

I am so grateful and thankful for my wonderful car

Learning Tools to Manifest Are Just Skills

Skills encompass everything we learn throughout our lives, from the simplest tasks to more complex abilities. If you reflect on it, even actions like using the toilet or eating with utensils are skills we acquired over time. We weren't born doing these. Watching my two-year-old grandchildren learn reminds me of all the things we had to master that now feel like second nature, and we rarely think about the fact that we had to learn those skills. It's essential to be gentle with yourself during the learning process. Just as we wouldn't scold a toddler for not holding a fork correctly or for having an accident, it's important not to criticize yourself as you develop new skills. With practice comes improvement; the more you engage with a skill, the more automatic it becomes.

As we explore this page, I want to revisit the metaphor of the GPS system, which I will refer to throughout this book. One common observation I've made over the years with many individuals is that they often lack a clear understanding of what they truly want in life; instead, they are more aware of what they don't want. Without a clear sense of direction, it's akin to being a boat adrift on the ocean, tossed by waves from one direction to another. We may only begin to paddle when we approach danger, and in our panic, we might find ourselves caught in a whirlpool—revolving in circles with no idea how to break free until the winds shift.

At times, we might surrender to the currents, allowing them to take us wherever they may lead. In other instances, we may attempt to navigate in one direction, only to find no land in sight, prompting us to turn back. Before we know it, we're lost in the vast ocean, feeling paralyzed and uncertain of how to find our way back. In these moments, we may call out to God for help. However, if we remain unclear about our destination, God might send a massive boat to rescue us, only for us to reject it because it doesn't align with our preconceived notions of how assistance should appear. That new vessel may seem intimidating, making it more comfortable to remain in our small boat—at least there, we know what to expect.

This reflects how our brains function: we often cling to familiar situations, even if they are unhealthy, because they feel safe. Change can be daunting, and we may fixate on particular outcomes, such as hoping for a specific person to rescue us. When that doesn't happen, feelings of rejection and abandonment can resurface, echoing our childhood experiences.

Interestingly, neuroscience reveals that our brains can become "hooked" on certain thoughts, especially when we try to suppress them. For example, if I say, "Don't think about a yellow rabbit," your mind immediately conjures up an image of a yellow rabbit. This phenomenon occurs because the brain doesn't process negatives effectively; it focuses on the object of the instruction—the yellow rabbit—rather than the act of not thinking about it.

This tendency to get "stuck" in repetitive thinking is often linked to the brain's limbic system, particularly the amygdala and the prefrontal cortex. The amygdala processes emotions and can trigger a fight-or-flight response when faced with perceived threats, making it easier for us to dwell on negative thoughts or fears. The prefrontal cortex, responsible for higher-order functions like decision-making and impulse control, can struggle to override these emotional responses. When we feel overwhelmed or uncertain, the amygdala can dominate, leading to cycles of anxiety and rumination.

Another relevant aspect is the role of the anterior cingulate cortex (ACC), which is involved in error detection and emotional regulation. When we become aware of a conflict between our desires and our current circumstances, the ACC activates, signaling the need for adjustment. However, if we are not clear about what we want, this area can become inefficient, leading to confusion and indecision.

Moreover, the concept of neuroplasticity—how our brains adapt and reorganize themselves—plays a crucial role in this process. The more we practice identifying our desires and making decisions based on them, the stronger the neural pathways associated with those thoughts and behaviors become. Conversely, if we continually focus on what we don't want, we reinforce those patterns, making it harder to shift our mindset.

I invite you to gain clarity about what you truly want in your life. As you become more precise in your desires, you'll be better equipped to establish boundaries around what you don't want. This clarity will guide you in determining the direction you need to take to achieve your goals. Moreover, it will empower you to make specific requests in your prayers, trusting that God will bring what is best for you.

Understanding that the "who" in our lives is ultimately up to God is crucial. If we ask specifically for what we want, we can trust that it will unfold for our good. With clarity, we can discern whether the people or opportunities that come our way align with our true desires.

Many individuals struggle with identifying their wants because they have never been taught this essential skill. This doesn't reflect poorly on you; rather, it's a skill that can be learned and developed.

Consider this scenario: you arrive at a restaurant and choose the first one you see. Upon sitting down, you realize it's an Italian restaurant, but you don't want Italian food. Reluctantly, you choose to eat anyway. In another situation, you might be dining with friends who insist you try the prime rib, even though you dislike it. You acquiesce, only to discover you don't enjoy it at all.

Alternatively, you might visit your favorite restaurant, only to find they're out of your preferred dish. Not wanting to hurt anyone's feelings, you order something else, but when it arrives, it fails to satisfy. You've spent money on a meal you didn't want, all in the name of politeness. This tendency to please others often stems from codependency, where you prioritize others' preferences over your own soul.

Now imagine a different approach: you arrive at a restaurant and say, "I don't know what I want; let me look at the menu." If nothing appeals to you, you might decide to explore another place. This choice shows growth in clarity because you understand what you don't want.

Let's say you then realize you want seafood. You research nearby seafood restaurants, checking their ratings and menus. Once you find one that offers your favorite dishes, you enjoy a satisfying meal and leave excited to share your experience with friends. This illustrates what it means to gain clarity in your desires.

Remember, this is a practice, and practice leads to permanence. It's also true that some people seek constant variety, chasing dopamine fixes when they grow bored. We'll delve deeper into this later, but for now, keep in mind our goal: to gain increasing clarity about what we truly want, ensuring that both God and those around us understand our desires. Embrace the journey of learning and celebrate your progress along the way.

Here is an exercise to get clear about what we want:

1. First, write down what you do not want in your life. Examples could be: debt, toxic relationships, anger, binge eating, depression, anxiety, etc.

    Example: I don't want abusive relationships. I don't want debt. I don't want fear. I don't want to be overweight.

_____

_____

_____

_____

_____

_____

_____

_____

_____

2. Second, rewrite each of your "I don't want" statements opposite. What would be the opposite of that statement? Then, write it.

    Example: I want money. I want to be debt-free. I want to feel joy. I want peace. I want healthy people in my life. I want a healthy relationship.

_____

_____

_____

_____

_____

_____

_____

3. Third, write even more clearly each of the above statements.

    Example: I want money to flow in my life with ease to give, keep, spend, and cycle. I want to be debt-free, making about $5k a month with a purposeful job I love. I want to feel joy, and I will let myself have fun. I want peace and will use healthy tools to get there. I want healthy people in my life and will allow myself to say no when it doesn't fit for me. I want a healthy relationship and will put boundaries up for people who choose not to be healthy.

_____

_____

_____

_____

_____

_____

_____

_____

Here are a few of my favorite skills you can practice. Some are ones I came up with, and some I have learned along the way that help me and my clients.

1. Identifying and writing down daily gratitude lists.
2. Make a to-do list with you on one side of the page and God on the other. Give God as many tasks as you are ready to relinquish to get help and guidance. Notice what He does and write it out.
3. Write out at least 3 things you want as if you already had them 3 times per day (3 times in the morning, 3 times in the afternoon, and 3 times in the evening).
4. Meditate for at least 10 minutes twice a day, starting with the intention of what you would like (healing, blessings, financial freedom, a job, something for someone else, etc.).
5. Exercise for 15 to 20 minutes a day. If you have health issues, break this down to 3-minute exercises 3 times per day.
6. Write down a scripture a day, read it, and memorize it.

7. Notice the abundance of the world all around you. Examples: Look outside at the tree and try to count the leaves. You couldn't, right? There is an abundance. Count the hairs on your head. Abundance!

8. Catch your negative thoughts and say a catchphrase to release them:
   a. I don't have to know to let it go.
   b. Silly brain, let my thoughts fall away like rain.
   c. Little thoughts, it's time you forgot.
   d. Past, Past, go away, life is better today.
   e. I will know when I let it go.
   f. One I heard from another person: Silly mind, I give you to the Divine.
   g. Time is always on my side.
   h. Every day, I'm getting better.

9. When you get stuck in your brain on something negative, write out 16 positives to help you change it. Neuroscience says it takes about 16 seconds to shift from negative to positive.

10. Look back at a situation you feel is stuck in your mind, as if you are the observer watching above or from the sidelines. Noticing with curiosity and love, ask yourself what you could have done differently to make a better outcome. Don't judge yourself or the other person, but allow yourself to replay this with the new information and see what happens.

11. Share your blessings at the end of the day using the 3x3 method: Three great things that happened for you and three things you did well.

All of these are skills that you can practice to strengthen your brain connections and manifest more easily.

The Role of Emotions and Memory

Question: How do emotions influence the encoding and retrieval of memories?

_____

_____

Exercise—Part 1: Reflect on a particularly emotional, preferably positive event, not a traumatic one, just an emotional one from your life. Write a detailed account of the event, focusing on the sensory details and emotions experienced. Consider how these emotions have strengthened your memory of the event. Notice how applying this can help you enhance visualization practices by incorporating positive emotions.

_____

_____

_____

_____

Exercise—Part 2: Now think of a stressful memory. Again, not traumatic, just give yourself permission to look at the event curiously. Write a detailed account of the event, focusing on the sensory details and emotions experienced. Consider how these emotions have strengthened your memory of the event.

_____

_____

_____

_____

There may be certain past experiences you'd like to transform in order to release the emotions tied to them. Fortunately, there are effective techniques available that can help alter the way your brain processes these memories by introducing new emotions. One approach involves revisiting a memory you'd like to reshape and allowing yourself to engage in genuine laughter, even if it feels forced. This deep, hearty laughter can significantly lessen the intensity of the feelings associated with a challenging event.

Another valuable method for recontextualizing a memory is to visualize yourself handling it in a positive manner—essentially, imagining the scenario as you wish it had unfolded. This practice, known as rescripting, encourages you to invest emotional energy and excitement into the visualization, which can help alleviate the negative feelings you previously experienced. This is one of my favorite tools to help clients use to rewire the brain.

My clients often say that as they work using these kinds of tools, they are able to release negative experiences much quicker, especially as they tap into the knowledge that all of these things are skills.

While these techniques can be effective, you may find it beneficial to work alongside a skilled coach or counselor. Remember, it is entirely possible to rewire and diffuse emotional responses in the brain, a central theme of our discussion here.

Additional Interactive Questions and Exercises

Daily Mindfulness Practice

Question: How can mindfulness meditation enhance your brain function and support your manifestation goals?

_____

_____

_____

_____

_____

_____

Exercise 1: Mindfulness Meditation

Dedicate 10 to 15 minutes each day to the practice of mindfulness meditation. For those who are new to focused meditation, it can be helpful to begin by placing a candle or any object of your choice at eye level. I have a few clients who like to have a picture of Jesus that they focus on. This will serve as your point of concentration. Start by focusing on your breath, inhaling deeply into your heart space, and observing your thoughts without judgment. When thoughts arise, gently release them from your mind, imagining them as leaves drifting in the wind or clouds floating across the sky.

If you find your mind racing, try producing a humming sound or a deep "amen" from your diaphragm to help ground yourself. Many people discover that meditating outdoors and concentrating on a tree or natural element enhances their experience even further. After each meditation session, take a moment to jot down any insights or shifts in your mental state, as well as your emotional feelings. Consider how mindfulness supports your ability to remain focused on your goals and aspirations.

If you resonate with my experience, you might also navigate life with an ADHD brain. I've discovered remarkable insights through the practice of clearing mind meditations. Initially, I believed that guided meditations were the only option for me, and I focused solely on that method for years. I even taught others that some individuals simply needed guided sessions, and that was perfectly acceptable and still helpful. However, research has unveiled that practicing clear mind meditations can lead to significant changes in the brain.

I started by focusing on an object, and it may have only lasted a few seconds, being in a clear mind, but then I worked up to a minute, three minutes, and then before I knew it, twenty minutes. Wow, it felt liberating. Like I turned on a superpower I didn't know I had access to, and now I can often find myself with a clear mind. It is so liberating and freeing. Now, I don't want you to get the idea I never deal with the ADD brain tendencies, but it is much better and more manageable. Just remember to be patient with yourself.

Engaging in these meditations increases gray matter, enhancing both learning and memory. They strengthen neural connections, improve focus and concentration, and help alleviate stress and anxiety. Additionally, they promote better sleep and can even lower blood pressure. Think of it as a workout for your brain, building mental resilience and providing clarity about your aspirations in life. It truly is an incredible journey.

Don't be discouraged if it takes several attempts to become proficient at clearing your mind. Start with just one minute each day, gradually adding an extra minute until you reach 10 or 15 minutes. Observe the transformation that occurs. Remember, this is a skill, much like learning to ride a bicycle—it requires time and practice, but the benefits for both mind and body are astounding.

Some may feel hesitant about the term "meditation," fearing it leads them away from God's teachings. However, the Bible encourages us to meditate on His Word day and night. It also invites us to pause and listen. How can we hear His guidance if our minds are constantly racing? It is in the stillness, beyond the chaotic thoughts, that we can attune ourselves to the gentle voice that offers the direction we seek.

I remember discovering years ago, through a reading I came across, how churches used to have more silent times—a time with no music, just tuning in, listening, and being still. Some denominations still practice this, but it is few and far between. We have created the need for constant noise and action so much that we tend to feel uncomfortable at first as we try to sit in silence. Think how much better the whole world would be if we learned to sit in stillness and silence... that's peace at its purest essence. It is a practice I've grown to love that brings so much peace, too. Reflect on the practice.

_____

_____

_____

_____

_____

_____

Exercise 2: Meta Prayer

When I was the sickest after having COVID-19 in November of 2020, I was struggling to find hope. I was so mad at my body. I always had a "suck it up and drive on" attitude, but that wasn't working for me. The more I pushed, the more I was down physically, mentally, and emotionally. It was exhausting, and I felt defeated, which only added to feeling depressed and almost hopeless. I even told God at one point, "I can't do this anymore, this is too hard." I was in so much pain from the myalgia and daily migraines, not to mention my brain wasn't working right. I was having word-finding problems and memory problems. I would stutter and just feel like a fraction of the person I used to be. I later found out I had a brain injury, possibly from the migraines or COVID; they couldn't tell how, but the scans showed it. I had just applied for my doctorate degree in Psychology the summer before and was hoping to start in January. Those dreams were all gone now, too. Facing all the heaviness of loss plus health issues felt insurmountable. When I finally surrendered to God, He began directing me by reminding me of the Meta Prayer and led me to use it on the parts of me I hated. He also guided me to contact Dr. Amen's Clinic. Seeing my brain scans made me feel a bit more compassion for myself. Then I began incorporating my healing journey by doing micro steps like you would with a person who had a stroke. I had worked with thousands of people over the years who had brain injuries and strokes, so I knew I had to give myself more grace, like I would them.

There are several ways you can use the Meta Prayer. Here are a few:

1. Imagine the version of you who's sick or feeling hopeless and sends love, waving your hand toward another version of you in that state, saying, "May You Have Love, May You Have Peace, May You Have Wisdom." Then say, "May I Have Love, May I Have Peace, May I Have Wisdom." Do this as many times as you need until you begin to feel better or notice the image of you and that person changes.

   This form of prayer activates your compassion centers, seeing you and them in a better place. Isn't that cool! I have worked with countless people who have used this in relationships that were struggling, who talked about the other person shifting and changing different things in themselves, and feeling more like they were more open to the other person as well. You may interchange the words and continue to say these meta prayer words using different words at least three times for the other person and three times for yourself, shifting different words until you feel better. Then, leave it to God because it actually is a prayer.

2. Another way you can use the Meta Prayer is by imagining someone who has hurt you or whom you're upset with. When you use the Meta Prayer for someone else, you can do it in the following ways: "May You Have Love, May You Have Peace, May You Have Hope." Then say, "May I Have Love, May I Have Peace, May I Have Hope." Do this as many times as you need until you begin to feel better or notice the image change to a more positive posture. It's a form of prayer and compassion for parts of you that are stuck or hurting.

The Meta Prayer is very interesting and may seem a bit crazy if you've never heard of it, but I assure you, it has actually been researched as well. I first learned about the Meta Prayer from a Mindfulness training I went through years ago through PESI for my license. When you do the Meta Prayer, it affects an area at the top back part of your brain called the prefrontal cortex and the posterior cingulate. These parts of the brain actually help with reflective thought and self-awareness, so we are in a higher order when we're in that meta prayer mode. It also affects other areas of the brain, but it's super interesting to think about how something like this could not only create more mindfulness but also help us heal in different ways. It helps stop racing thoughts in the limbic system and also helps us with our relationships.

Conclusion

Grasping the intricacies of brain science offers profound insights into how our thoughts and beliefs influence our reality. By delving into brain functions, embracing positive thinking and visualization techniques, enhancing memory, and integrating mindfulness along with healthy lifestyle choices, you can tap into the remarkable power of your mind to bolster your manifestation goals. Engaging with interactive questions and exercises will deepen your comprehension and application of these principles, allowing your thoughts and beliefs to transform your life in harmony with your highest aspirations. The Meta Prayer played a crucial role in fostering compassion for myself throughout my healing journey, and I continue to incorporate it into my daily practice as well as teach clients to use it. This powerful method not only nurtures self-love but also helps develop the mindfulness areas of the brain in a deeply spiritual manner.

Reflection Notes

CHAPTER 5

Traumas, Tragedies, and Setbacks: Moving Through Pain Into Purpose

It's often the unexpected blows in life—the phone call in the middle of the night, the doctor's diagnosis, the job that vanishes without warning, the fire that burns not just our belongings but the sense of safety we once knew—that shake us to the core. We don't choose trauma. We don't ask for tragedy. We don't volunteer for setbacks. But somehow, these moments mark us. They test what we believe. They press into every place of pain we've kept hidden. And if we're honest, they can leave us wondering where God is in it all. I remember struggling with this concept in my twenties and not only for my life but for the lives of the people I worked with. The ultimate question often appeared: "Why would a good God who is all-powerful let this happen?" I've sat with countless people who carried silent pain so heavy it threatened to take them under. The women who lost their children. The people rebuilding after a brain injury. Families, torn apart by house fires and financial ruin, or divorce. The invisible wounds of anxiety, PTSD, chronic illness, or grief that lingers far longer than anyone expects. I've lived my own trauma, too—fighting for my life after COVID ravaged my brain and body, dealing with loss, and learning to accept a new norm as I worked toward healing, learning to breathe again when the world I knew no longer existed. I have faced my share of traumas and tribulations: childhood trauma, loss of dreams from an unhealthy marriage, loss of my military career after having blood clots in my lungs, loss of control when my daughter was diagnosed with a life-threatening illness that almost took her life, loss of people, loss of a house through a fire with not only my belongings but heirlooms my family brought over from their motherland, and the list could go on and on.

And yet... even here, God meets us.

Even when our backs are against the wall and we're crawling through the valley of the shadow, there is a breath of heaven that whispers, "I am still with you. I have not left. I love you, I will restore you." There are those among us who believe we accepted or agreed or chose some contracts before we came to earth to practice them in our lives. Working with thousands of people who have gone through trauma, I can't see or believe anyone would make an agreement to come to earth to cause pain to oneself or others. I don't find anything that lines up with this in the Word of God, and in all of my seeking, God has not revealed this to me. I do, however, believe that we can find hope and guidance in God's Word when we are going through these things. I also believe the Word of God is clear in seeking wise counsel. You don't have to go through these things alone. A book that really spoke to my heart, when dealing with tragedies that held no real answers, is *When God Doesn't Make Sense* by Dr. James Dobson. I would highly encourage anyone going through struggles like these to read this book.

What the Bible Says About Pain, Loss, and Restoration

"...to bestow on them a crown of beauty instead of ashes, the oil of joy instead of mourning, and a garment of praise instead of a spirit of despair. They will be called oaks of righteousness, a planting of the Lord for the display of his splendor." — Isaiah 61:3 (NIV)

Even when it feels like everything has burned down—our hopes, our dreams, our sense of self—God promises beauty in exchange for our ashes. This isn't poetic fluff. It's His divine restoration plan in action. What we thought was the end becomes the beginning of something sacred.

"Those who sow with tears will reap with songs of joy. Those who go out weeping, carrying seed to sow, will return with songs of joy, carrying sheaves with them." — Psalm 126:5-6 (NIV)

God sees every tear. None are wasted. What you water with your weeping, He will harvest in joy. There's a return coming. A divine exchange of pain for praise, sorrow for song.

Scripture does not ignore our suffering. God's Word acknowledges it—and offers healing in the midst of it.

"The Lord is close to the brokenhearted and saves those who are crushed in spirit." — Psalm 34:18 (NIV)

"He will wipe every tear from their eyes. There will be no more death or mourning or crying or pain..." — Revelation 21:4 (NIV)

"...by His wounds we are healed." — Isaiah 53:5 (NIV)

"I will repay you for the years the locusts have eaten..." — Joel 2:25 (NIV)

"Trust in the Lord with all your heart and lean not on your own understanding..." — Proverbs 3:5-6 (NIV)

Brain Science and the Impact of Trauma

Our brains are masterfully designed to survive. When we face trauma, our brains react by prioritizing safety above all else. Over time, if unaddressed, this survival mode becomes our default.

- **Amygdala**: Becomes hyperactive, causing hypervigilance, intrusive memories, and fear-based reactions.
- **Hippocampus**: Memory center. Trauma blurs time, making past events feel like present dangers.
- **Prefrontal Cortex**: Underfunctions, impairing rational thinking, decision-making, and emotional regulation.
- **Neuroplasticity**: Offers hope. The brain is capable of forming new pathways of healing and peace.

Long-term trauma also disrupts hormone balances, raising cortisol, depleting dopamine, and affecting sleep and immunity.

God's Design for Healing

Healing is not just a process; it's a promise. God created our bodies and minds with the resilience to recover and the Spirit to guide us through it. Healing looks different for everyone. Sometimes, it's instant. Other times, it's a journey of faith and micro steps.

"After Job had prayed for his friends, the Lord restored his fortunes and gave him twice as much as he had before." — Job 42:10 (NIV)

Your restoration may not look like Job's, but it will carry the fingerprints of heaven.

Counseling, Brain Health, and Faith-Based Tools That Help

To help people move from a place of defeat to determination and healing, I teach and use integrated tools such as:

- **Daily W.I.N. Practice (What's Important Now)**: This method, developed by football coach Lou Holtz, keeps you focused on what matters most each day. Ask yourself, "What's important now?" Then act on that one thing. Whether it's resting, praying, drinking water, or calling a friend, it brings focus and clarity in the fog of trauma. Micro choices create macro change.

- **The T.H.I.N.K. Method**: When your thoughts spiral, ask: "Is it True? Is it Helpful? Is it Inspiring? Is it Necessary? Is it Kind?" This filters out fear-driven lies and returns you to truth and love-based thinking. The T.H.I.N.K. method has been used by many counselors, coaches, and ministers to help shift our minds and was used in the anti-bully campaign put out by Character Education Programs; however, it truly goes back to the fruits of the spirit.

- **Safe Space Visualization**: Imagine the most beautiful place you have ever been and allow yourself to feel God's peace, light filling up the room and shining down on you as if God would say, "I love you, you are important, you are enough, you are worthy, I am here with you," filling your body with God's love and light from the top of your head all down your body. Fill the place with calming sounds, Jesus, angels, scriptures, and items that make you feel safe. Retreat here in your mind when overwhelmed.

- **Reset Routine**: Every time your anxiety spikes or your energy crashes, do a mini-reset: pause, breathe, stretch, hydrate, and refocus.

- **Grief Mapping**: Draw a circle and write your loss in the center. Around it, list everything it affected—identity, routines, dreams. Then, around those, write how God is helping you reclaim or reframe each area. This allows your grief to move, rather than stagnate.

- **Prayer & Tapping (EFT)**: Gently tap specific acupressure points while praying through the pain. Speak God's truth aloud: "Even though I feel fear, I trust You are with me." This calms the body and anchors the Spirit.

You can find these exercises and some guided meditations for free on my website at https://msha.ke/warriorheartxo#links-2

Real-Life Examples of Trauma

Pain wears many faces:

- The mother, burying her child
- The caregiver, losing themselves in compassion fatigue
- The brain injury survivor, learning to speak again
- The believer, trying to hold on after losing everything in a fire
- The betrayed spouse, navigating shattered trust

Every person's trauma is unique, but God's healing power is universal.

God's Way Forward

No matter how shattered you feel, there is a path forward. God is not only present in the pain—He leads you out of it.

"And we know that in all things God works for the good of those who love Him..." — Romans 8:28 (NIV)

You may not understand it all now, lean not unto your own understanding as His word says, but healing doesn't require perfect understanding. It requires trust.

Expanded Action Steps for Healing and Moving Forward

1. **Acknowledge the pain without shame**: Be honest. Say it. Write it. Name the hurt. See yourself handing each one to Jesus as you release them, like handing over a lump of coal and allowing Jesus to replace it with a diamond.

2. **Cry out to God honestly**: Your raw emotions are welcome. God can handle your emotions and questions. Sometimes, doing art will help. For others, you may go out to a creek and throw rocks with frustration, pain, and anguish, releasing them from the body.

3. **Daily W.I.N. step**: Tune into your spirit and ask God what's one thing I can do right now that helps me get closer to healing. Choose one healing act each day (e.g., call a friend, read a verse, walk in the sun).

4. **Journal your grief story**: What was lost? What was learned? Where do you see glimmers of God?

5. **Practice deep breathing + a breath prayer**: Inhale: "Jesus, You are near." Exhale: "I am safe in You."

6. **Use the T.H.I.N.K. tool when overwhelmed**: Guide your thoughts back to truth and love.

7. **Reset every hour**: Move your body, sip water, speak scripture, look up to the sky.

8. **Worship even in the weeping**: Let praise shift your atmosphere. What can you be grateful for today? It doesn't mean you are not hurting, it just balances the fact that we do have good in our lives, even in the midst of tragedy.

9. **Speak life out loud**: Declare healing, hope, and restoration over yourself. The Word of God says, "Call those things that are not as though they were." Claiming your power and healing is not denying pain but choosing faith that all things will work together for your good.

10. **Keep showing up**: On hard days, just doing one small thing is enough. Healing is still happening. Sometimes, that one small thing is rest, other times, it's setting a timer for allowing yourself to grieve a few times a day, and then doing one task towards what you need to get done. Life doesn't stop when tragedies hit, but we can find ways to process them a bit more easily by taking some action steps.

Conclusion

Trauma, tragedy, and setbacks are part of the human experience, but they are not the end of the story. The God who formed you also formed a path to your healing. Through faith, scripture, brain science, and practical tools, you can move from pain to purpose. Your wounds can become holy ground. You are being rewired by grace. You are not alone. Healing is already unfolding.

Reflection & Processing Prompts

Use these journal prompts to go deeper:

1. What recent trauma, loss, or setback has left you feeling stuck?

_____

_____

_____

_____

2. What areas of your life feel most affected?

_____

_____

_____

_____

3. What does your grief need to say today?

_____

_____

_____

_____

4. How have you seen God's hand—even slightly—in the midst of your pain?

_____

_____

_____

5. What's one small W.I.N. step can you take today?

_____

_____

_____

6. Which T.H.I.N.K. filter question challenged you the most? Why?

_____

_____

_____

_____

7. What scripture speaks to your heart right now? Write it out and declare it.

_____

_____

_____

_____

8. If you could hear God whisper one thing over you right now, what would you want Him to say?

_____

_____

_____

_____

9. What do you want your life to look like?

_____

_____

_____

You are healing. You are not beyond hope. God's breath is in your lungs, and His promise is over your pain.

Reflection Notes

CHAPTER 6

Aligning Your Thoughts with God's Word

Aligning your thoughts with God's Word is a profound journey that harmonizes your mind, spirit, and actions with divine principles. Engaging in this practice can greatly enhance your capacity to manifest your desires in alignment with God's Will. This chapter delves into techniques for aligning your thoughts with biblical scripture, highlighting the significance of meditation and prayer in shaping your mindset. Additionally, it offers inspiring case studies and testimonials that illustrate the power of successful alignment in transforming lives.

Techniques for Aligning Thoughts with Biblical Scriptures

Aligning your thoughts with scriptures involves immersing in God's Word and allowing its truths to permeate your mind and influence your thinking. Here are some effective techniques to help you achieve alignment.

1. **Daily Scripture Reading:** Consistent reading of the Bible is fundamental. Dedicate time each day to read and reflect on scripture. Start with passages that resonate with current life circumstances. Remember to make this curious and light, not like schoolwork that has to be done, but more like an invitation to spend time with God.

2. **Memorization:** Select scriptures that inspire you and commit them to memory. Write down a scripture on a post-it and place it on your mirror. Just one a day for a week. Recite one scripture daily for memorizing, and especially recite it during times of doubt and stress.

3. **Prayer Time:** Set aside some time to pray about issues in your life. Remember, prayer is a conversation with God. I love the scripture that

says, "Pray without ceasing." In other words, you can just have a conversation all day long with God. However, during your prayer time, get specific about the things you want to leave with God. Ask God to show you He's there and working on your behalf. I like to start my mornings with thankfulness for what God has done for me and blessings, and then I write out things I want to leave with God to take care of. The end of the day is a great time to think about prayers that have been answered throughout the day and anything that hasn't been worked out, saying something like "I know you are working that out." Then in the morning, I revisit my answered prayers and blessings from the day before, before writing out my new list of things I want to ask God's help with. The more you rehearse the answered prayers and blessings, the more it helps us remember He is working things out for our good.

4. **Meditate on a Scripture:** Choose a scripture you can meditate on for a week. Close your eyes and repeat the scripture in your mind, allowing it to resonate deeply. Reflect on the meaning and even ask God during your meditations to reveal the meanings and how they fit into your life now. Then, journal about it.

5. **Journal:** Having a prayer and praise journal can be amazing. Write out your praises first, at least five. Then, write out answers to prayers. Then, write out prayers that you want God to work on. I even write out things like a to-do list to give to God, and it's amazing how much He answers.

Case Studies and Testimonials of Successful Alignment

Numerous individuals have experienced profound transformations by aligning their thoughts with God's Word. The following are case studies and testimonials to serve as a powerful testimony of the impact of this practice. These are not meant to represent any particular person and have been used to represent a general look at how people have used scripture to change their lives.

Case Study 1: Sarah's Journey to Peace

Sarah struggled with anxiety and negative thoughts for years. Despite trying various coping mechanisms, she couldn't find lasting peace. One day, she decided to immerse herself in prayer. Philippians 4:6-7 says, "Do not be anxious about anything, but in every situation by prayer and petition with Thanksgiving, present your request to God. And the peace of God, which transcends all understanding, will guard your hearts and your minds in Christ Jesus."

Sarah began reading and meditating on the scripture daily. She also incorporated it into her prayers, asking God to replace her anxiety with peace. Over time, she noticed a significant reduction in her anxiety levels. Her thoughts became more positive and centered on God's promises. Today, Sarah testifies that prayerful conversations with God have brought her unparalleled peace and joy.

Case Study 2: John's Transformation Through Affirmations

John faced self-doubt and feelings of inadequacy in his career. A friend suggested he start using affirmations based on scripture to boost his confidence. John chose Philippians 4:13, "I can do all things through Christ who strengthens me," as his primary affirmation.

Every morning, John repeated this affirmation, believing in its truth. He also wrote it down and placed it around his workspace as a constant reminder. Gradually, his self-doubt diminished, and he felt more empowered to take on challenges at work. John's performance improved, and he even received a promotion. He attributes his success to the power of aligning his thoughts with God's Word.

Case Study 3: Maria's Healing Through Meditation and Prayer

Maria was diagnosed with a chronic illness that left her feeling hopeless and depressed. She decided to return to meditation and prayer for solace. She began meditating on Psalm 103:2-3, "Praise the Lord my soul and forget not all his benefits who forgives all your sins and heals all your diseases."

Maria spent time each day meditating on these verses, visualizing God's healing power at work in her body. She also prayed fervently, asking God for strength and healing. She experienced not only a significant improvement in her physical health but also a deep sense of peace and hope. She shares that aligning her thoughts with God's Word through meditation and prayer was instrumental in her healing journey.

Case Study 4: David's Overcoming Fear with Scripture

David battled fear and insecurity, especially when speaking in public. He decided to align his thoughts with God's Word by focusing on Isaiah 41:10, "So do not fear, for I am with you; do not be dismayed, for I am your God. I will strengthen you and help you, I will uphold you with my righteous right hand."

David memorized this verse and repeated it before every public speaking engagement. He also incorporated it into his prayers, asking God for courage and strength. As he continued this practice, David's fear diminished, and he became more confident and effective in his speaking. He confidently shares his testimony of how aligning his thoughts with God's Word helped him overcome his fears.

Interactive Questions and Exercises

1. Reflecting on Personal Testimonials

Question: What stories of faith and transformation inspire you the most?

_____

_____

Exercise: Research and read two or three testimonials of people who have successfully aligned their thoughts with God's Word and experienced transformation. Write a reflection on how those stories inspire you and what lesson you can apply to your own life.

_____

_____

_____

_____

2. Sharing Your Journey

Question: How can sharing your experience strengthen your faith and encourage others?

_____

_____

Exercise: Write a short testimonial about a time when aligning your thoughts with God's Word made a significant difference in your life. Share this story with a friend or a faith community. Reflect on how sharing our journey impacts your faith and inspires others.

_____

_____

_____

_____

3. Practical Application of Biblical Stories

Question: Which biblical stories resonate with your current life situation?

_____

_____

Exercise: Identify a biblical story that mirrors a challenge or goal in your life.

Study the story in depth and reflect on the actions and faith of the characters involved. Write down practical steps you can take to emulate their faith and align your actions with God's Will. The Bible is all about metaphors, teaching life lessons. It was meant to give us guidance in having a blessed, abundant life, not to use it as a way to beat up on ourselves or others.

_____

_____

_____

_____

4. Create a Scripture-Based Vision Board

Question: How can a vision board help you focus on aligning your thoughts with God's Word?

_____

_____

Exercise: Create a vision board that includes your favorite scripture, related images, and affirmations. Place it somewhere you will see it daily. Use this visual tool as a reminder to keep your thoughts aligned with God's Word.

_____

_____

_____

_____

5. Strengthening Your Faith Through Community

Question: How can engaging with a faith community support your journey of alignment?

_____

_____

Exercise: Join a Bible study group or faith-based community. Share your goals and experiences with aligning your thoughts with God's Word. Participate actively in discussions and activities. What step will you take to engage in community? What groups are available to try out?

_____

_____

_____

_____

Throughout my life, the church has held a special significance for me. As a young girl, it was a sanctuary where I felt safe and loved. This sense of belonging is still important to me. I cherish the fellowship with others, even though I've faced my share of challenges within various church communities, and at times, I've found that certain groups just don't resonate with me. I've also experienced trauma from people in the church who call themselves Christian. I remind myself that's not God, nor does it please God. I have also worked with many people over the years who've been harmed by people of almost any religion you can think of, as well as those who don't believe in God. So, when people try to categorize hurt from a denomination, religion, work environment, or culture, again, I say that's not God, that's people. Nonetheless, I believe that surrounding ourselves with like-minded individuals who uplift and inspire us on our journeys is one of the most valuable tools we can possess. It helps us stay focused and encourages us to strive toward our goals. If a particular church or group doesn't feel like the right fit for you, don't hesitate to seek out another community that aligns better with your spirit. Nowadays, there are even online faith-based groups that can offer connection and support. Plus, the power of community prayer can have an astounding effect. I truly believe in the power of community prayer. Matthew 18:20 (NIV): "For where two or three gather in my name, there am I with them."

Conclusion

Aligning your thoughts with God's Word is a transformative practice that has the potential to reshape both your mind and your life. By immersing yourself in scripture, utilizing affirmations, engaging in meditation, and participating in prayer, you can harmonize your thoughts with divine truths. The interactive questions and exercises included in this chapter are designed to enhance your understanding and application of these principles. Reflecting on your faith, creating personalized affirmations, visualizing through scripture, and sharing your journey with others will help you remain dedicated and inspired as you walk this path. Remember that God's Word is a wellspring of wisdom, guidance, and transformation, ready to renew your mind and align your reality with His Will.

Reflection Notes

CHAPTER 7

Practical Applications of Brain Science

Harnessing the power of brain science can profoundly enhance our ability to manifest our desires and goals. By understanding how our brains work and applying specific techniques, we can align our thoughts and actions with the outcomes we seek. This chapter explores methods for leveraging brain science, using manifestation visualization techniques supported by neuroscience, and effectively creating new vision boards.

Methods for Leveraging Brain Science and Manifestation

The human brain is a powerful tool that can be trained to support our goals and aspirations. One of my favorite sayings is "It's just a Program." I use this word regularly and have for years to remind my clients that everything you learned from womb to now... is just a programming. We are programmed from our family, school, church, community, TV, life experiences, and so much more. It's important to remember, as we delve deeper, that we can, in fact, change our lives by rewiring our brains. Some things are great to keep; you are not a total mess, you are a masterpiece in the making. I dive into deeper explorations of the brain in my upcoming book, *We Repeat What We Don't ReWire: It's a Program,* coming out in November 2025.

Here are several methods, grounded in brain science, that can help you manifest your desires more effectively:

1. **Neuroplasticity:**

   This is the brain's ability to reorganize itself by forming new neural connections throughout life. By consistently focusing on positive thoughts and desired outcomes. You can strengthen the neural pathways associated with those thoughts, making them more dominant. Positive affirmations and visualizing your goals daily can reinforce these neural pathways.

It wasn't long ago that we believed the brain lost its ability to change after a certain age, but today, we understand that this is far from true. I vividly recall the impact this knowledge had on the medical field during my early 20s. While working as the Director of the Alzheimer's unit in a nursing home, I witnessed the struggles of a 50-year-old woman who had suffered a stroke in her 30s. She faced significant challenges with mobility and speech, which was heartbreaking to witness. Do you really understand just how impactful this new research became for our whole world? Imagine one day believing this is just who you are, so you can change immensely. Today, we even know that with work you can mold personality tracks that you weren't quote unquote "born with, but that's for another discussion. It is important to know the brain is malleable, and we are only on the cusp of learning how much three decades later.

Fortunately, we now know that recovery is possible, even after some strokes. It simply requires time to rewire and adapt the brain, finding ways to navigate around the affected areas. While the extent of recovery can vary based on the severity of the stroke, I have seen individuals recover from strokes that left them with only subtle signs... often noticeable only when they are under stress or anxiety, as their bodies learn to navigate around the neural pathways. This is a testament to the brain's remarkable capacity for healing and adaptation. So, I often say if it's possible for one person, it is for another as well. For those who aren't dealing with recovery from a brain injury, even more hope is possible. I myself have a brain injury. That I have been navigating the last few years. Even as I rewrite parts of this book, I have to be gentle and forgiving of myself because the first time I self-published this book and paid a friend to edit it, I missed several errors. At first, I was frustrated with the level to which my brain was affected. Then, I remembered how far I have come in the past few years and what I would say to a client or friend.

2. Mindfulness Meditation:

Mindfulness meditation helps increase awareness and control over your thoughts. When practicing, you train your brain to stay focused on the present moment or on positive thoughts. Some people really struggle with this. I did. I also have struggled with ADHD. Also, for another and longer discussion, for those who struggle, here are a few tips that helped me immensely. After practicing for a period of time, I was actually so blown away that I could experience a clear mind.

Find an object parallel to your eyes. Stare at the object while concentrating on breathing in and out of your chest until everything around seems to fade and your eyes feel heavy. Allow your eyes to close. If thoughts come, let them float by or out of your head as if they are riding on a cloud. Give no judgment, just noticing. After several days of practicing this outside, using a tree as my focal point to begin, I remember how exciting it was to experience a clear mind for just a few seconds, and now I can do that practice much longer. Research shows that regular meditation can increase the thickness of the prefrontal cortex, which is associated with higher brain functions, such as concentration, decision-making, and planning.

3. Gratitude Practice:

Fostering a habit of gratitude can rewire your brain to emphasize the positive aspects of your life. When you consistently acknowledge and appreciate what you have, you activate the brain's reward system by triggering the release of dopamine and serotonin, which enhance your mood and overall well-being. Maintaining a gratitude journal—jotting down things you are thankful for each day—can profoundly influence your mindset and attract more positive experiences.

Throughout my years of working with thousands of individuals, I have encountered many who struggled to find anything good in their lives to be grateful for. I would encourage them to consider simple yet profound blessings: running water, a warm bed, electricity, the ability to walk or talk.

Initially, many would respond that these things did not feel significant or new. I would gently remind them that these are indeed blessings often overlooked because our brains tend to focus on what we lack or are vigilant about, rather than what we possess. This focus can lead to feelings of sadness, discontent, and even anxiety and depression. Unless we consciously train our minds to recognize the positives, we may miss out on acknowledging the abundance in our lives. This shift is crucial, as many of us are conditioned to be hyper-vigilant, constantly searching for potential dangers or what others have that we don't, instead of appreciating what is right in front of us.

4. **Positive Affirmations:**

Repeating positive affirmations can influence your subconscious mind and alter your neural pathways. Affirmations are positive statements that reinforce your goals and beliefs. You can shift your mindset and your thoughts with your desired reality by repeating them regularly. Examples of firming statements like "I am capable of achieving my goals" or "attracting success and abundance" can help reinforce beliefs. Your affirmative statement will wire your brain to go towards or away from things.

Henry Ford said, "Whether you think you can, or you think you can't, you're right."

5. **Habit Formation:**

Establishing positive habits can help integrate desired behaviors into your routine. The brain's basal ganglia play a crucial role and have habit formation. By consistently practicing positive behaviors, you create new neural pathways that make these behaviors automatic. Breaking down your goals into manageable steps and incorporating them into your daily routine can help solidify these habits. I am often reminded of my experience with sports. It took practice daily to learn how to get good at basketball, softball, volleyball, tennis, even roller skating, and riding a bicycle. In the military, we practiced shooting our weapons. Thank goodness..... Can you imagine handing guns to young people and just telling them to figure it out? It's up to you to decide if you really want something, and how to create practice times for your new habits.

Visualization Techniques Supported by Neuroscience

Visualization is a powerful technique that involves creating a mental image of your desired outcome. Supported by neuroscience, visualization can enhance performance, increase motivation, and accelerate goal achievement. Here are some effective visualization techniques:

1. **Detailed Mental Imagery:** When visualizing, it is essential to create a vivid and detailed mental image of your goal. Engage all of your senses to make the visualization as realistic as possible. The brain processes these vivid images similarly to real experiences, activating the same neural pathways. This can strengthen your belief in achieving your goal and prepare your brain for the actual experience.

2. **Future Self Visualization:** Imagine yourself having already achieved your goal. Visualize your future self—how do you feel and act, and how has your life changed? This technique helps the gap between your current self and your desired future, making it easier for your brain to accept and work towards this new reality. Your future self increases your motivation; it reinforces positive behaviors that align with your goals.

   James Allen said, "You are today where your thoughts have brought you; you will be tomorrow where your thoughts take you."

3. **Progress Visualization:** Instead of only visualizing the end goal, also visualize the steps needed to achieve it. This helps create a mental roadmap and prepares your brain for the journey ahead. By visualizing each step, you can reduce anxiety, increase confidence, and improve performance. This technique is particularly effective for complex or

long-term goals as it helps maintain focus and motivation throughout the process.

4. **Morning and Evening Visualization:** Incorporate visualization into your daily routine, particularly in the morning and evening—you start off with a positive tone, priming your brain for success. In the evening, reinforce your goals, which help to consolidate your mental imagery during sleep—a crucial time for memory and learning consolidation.

There is also research that says that these are prime times for your brain because we are in a state where the brain receives information into the subconscious or unconscious much more easily. When we first wake up in the morning, our brain waves move from Delta (sleep mode) into Theta (light sleep) and then to Alpha (state of relaxation and calmness). In the evenings, your brain begins to go back to a relaxed state again, shifting to alpha waves, which may help you prepare for sleep and is a great way to help train the brain during these times.

5. **Vision Boards:** Creating a vision board is a powerful tool for visualization. A vision board is a collage of images, words, and phrases that represent your goals and dreams. Posting it in a prominent location provides you with a constant visual reminder of what you are working towards. Creating a vision board also reinforces the goals in your mind and helps clarify intentions.

6. **Recording:** You can write down a script of the things that you want to happen in your life and then record yourself on your phone or a tape recorder and re-listen to the recordings in the morning, evening, and any other time you would like. It's really helpful to put in information that draws in your five senses, just like you would do a regular visualization. For many people who had difficulty visualizing without it being a guided meditation, this is a perfect tool. It's also great for those people who tend to be more verbal than visual.

How to Create and Use Vision Boards Effectively

First, I'd like to address the hesitation some people have regarding vision boards, often dismissing them as a new-age concept. Interestingly enough, my first encounter with a similar idea occurred in eighth grade during my Future Homemakers of America class. One of our projects involved creating a collage of career and life goals. Though it wasn't labeled a vision board, that's precisely what it was. We cut out pictures from magazines and glued them onto construction paper to depict the lives we aspired to lead.

There's nothing inherently wrong with crafting a vision board; in fact, many churches embrace this practice as well. I remember our church hosting a building fund project when I was a teenager, complete with a large image illustrating the proposed additions to the church and the funds needed for each area. Isn't that essentially a vision board? I encountered a similar concept when I managed a retail store where we outlined our goals in a flow chart format. Although it lacked pictures, it served the same purpose. Throughout my career, I've participated in various projects where we created visual marketing tools to convey the essence of upcoming events—another form of a vision board.

If the term "vision board" doesn't resonate with you, feel free to use an alternative like "goals board" or whatever term feels more comfortable. What I know for certain is that every vision board I've created has brought many of my aspirations to fruition. My first vision board was created in eighth grade and was accompanied by a recording of my hopes and dreams, which I listened to each night before bed. Almost everything I envisioned came true except for one particular desire. Ironically, not realizing it at the time, that desire not being answered turned out to be a blessing. It's amusing to reflect on how, as teenagers, we often dream of marrying someone who may not truly be our best match. As the song goes, "Sometimes I thank God for Unanswered Prayers" (Garth Brooks).

It's also fascinating how the marketing world has harnessed psychology to enhance sales. Advertisements function as vision boards, subtly influencing our minds as we watch TV or drive down the road. These commercials activate the reticular activating system in our brains, engaging all our senses while we are distracted, allowing messages to seep into our unconscious minds. This same principle applies in the medical field, where commercials for prescription drugs may resonate with you as you identify with various symptoms presented. Research shows it doesn't take much for us to connect with these messages, especially when they enter our minds at an unconscious level, subtly shaping our beliefs and perceptions. Most of the time, when you are watching TV or listening to the radio as you drive down the road, your brain is in a trance-type state.

I encourage you to be mindful of what you consume—whether through music, television, or other media. While it is natural to want to unwind, everything you expose yourself to primes your brain for certain thoughts and feelings. Ask yourself, "Is this really what I want to cultivate in my mind?"

Vision boards are visual representations of your goals and dreams designed to inspire and motivate you. Here's how to create and use vision boards effectively.

1. **Set Clear Goals:** Before creating your vision board, take time to reflect on your goals and desires. Be specific about what you wanted to achieve. Clarity is essential because it helps you focus your energy and effort on what truly matters.

2. **Gather Materials:** Collect materials that resonate with your goals. This can include magazines, photographs, printed images from the internet, inspirational quotes, and any other visual elements that represent your aspirations. You'll also need a board or a large piece of paper, glue, scissors, and markers. Write out positive statements, mantras, and scriptures to place on your board. If you have Canva, you can easily create and print out materials or the whole thing.

3. **Create Your Vision Board:** Take time to check in, pray, and ask yourself and God if there are any things you are seeking that don't feel in alignment with God's Word. Remember to check in if it's true or if you were programmed by this. Arrange the images and words on your

board in a way that feels meaningful to you. There's no right or wrong way to create a vision board. It's a personal and creative process. Take your time to ensure that each element on the board genuinely reflects who you are and your goals and dreams. I have Bible scriptures on mine.

4. **Place Your Vision Board in Sight:** Place your vision board in a location where you'll see it every day. This constant visual reminder will keep your goals fresh in your mind, reinforcing your commitment and motivation. Whether it's in your office, your bedroom, or any space where you spend a significant amount of time, make sure it's easily accessible. Each time you glance at it, it serves as a powerful cue, reminding you of what you're striving for, what you desire, and the dreams you hold dear. Your brain will respond to these cues, guiding you closer to your aspirations.

5. **Engage with Your Vision Board Daily**: Spend a few minutes every day, looking at your vision board. Use all your senses—see yourself having your desired outcome, while feeling the feelings, and smelling the smells. See the sights. Hear the sounds. Engage all your senses as if you already have everything you desire. You can remember to pray as you look at your vision board, something like "God help me to stay focused and intentional on creating my habits that bring these things to come," or "God help bring me the right resources and people to fulfill these dreams." This daily engagement can help your intentions stay more focused on your desired outcomes.

6. **Update Your Vision Board Regularly:** As you achieve your goals or as your aspirations shift, change, or evolve, you can update your vision board to reflect these changes. This ensures that your vision board remains relevant and continues to inspire you. Remember to celebrate the goals that you've achieved and set new ones to keep moving forward.

Exploring Neuroplasticity

Exercise: Choose one habit you want to develop and get better with, and one habit that you want to break. Pray and ask for God's guidance on how best to create this in your life. Inviting God's wisdom is always the best resource. Create a 30-day plan to reinforce the new habit while gradually reducing the old one. Reflect on the changes you observe and your behavior and mindset during this. Write out how the concepts of neuroplasticity can support you with these changes.

_____

_____

_____

_____

_____

Exercise: Keep a gratitude journal for one month. Each day, write down new things that you've learned as well as things that you are grateful for as you receive new blessings each day. Set an intention to list at least five a day. At the end of the month, review your entries and reflect on changes in your outlook and emotional well-being. Notice how this practice influences your ability to manifest positive outcomes because you get more of what you focus on. Reflect on the practice.

_____

_____

_____

_____

_____

Visualization Technique Supported by Neuroscience

Interactive Exercises:

Detailed Mental Imagery

Exercise: Select a specific goal and spend 10 minutes each day visualizing it in detail. Engage all of your senses to make the visualization as visible and vivid as possible. Write a description of your visualization, including what you see, hear, feel, smell, and taste. Reflect on how this practice affects your motivation and confidence.

_____

_____

_____

_____

Future Self Visualization

Exercise: Imagine yourself in the future, having already achieved your goal. Describe this future yourself in detail, focusing on your behaviors, feelings, and circumstances. Create a future-self journal where you write letters from your future self to your present self, offering advice and encouragement. Reflect on this practice.

_____

_____

_____

_____

Visualization with Affirmations

Exercise: Choose affirmations that align with your goal(s). Each day, visualize your goal while repeating your affirmations. For example, if your goal is to improve your health, you might visualize yourself as healthy and vibrant while repeating, "I am strong and full of energy" or "I can do all things through Christ, who gives me strength." Write out at least three to five affirmations for each of your goals.

_____

_____

_____

_____

_____

_____

_____

Combining Brain Science with Faith

Exercise: Choose a scripture that aligns with your manifestation goal. Combine this scripture with a brain science technique, such as visualization or affirmation. For example, you might visualize your goals while repeating Philippians 4:13, "I can do all things through Christ, who strengthens me." Reflect on how combining these practices strengthens your belief and manifestation efforts. Write down one or two scriptures that align with your goal.

_____

_____

_____

_____

_____

_____

_____

_____

Creating a Manifestation Routine

Exercise: Design a daily routine that includes practices such as gratitude, journaling, mindfulness, meditation, affirmations, visualization, and prayer. Write down your schedule and commit to following, tracking your progress, and reflecting on changes you observe in your mindset and goal achievement.

_____

_____

_____

_____

_____

_____

_____

_____

A Few of My Favorite Neuroscience Tools for Elevating Emotions

In the realm of neuroscience, there is a powerful principle: whatever you focus on, you will feel. This means that where your attention goes, your feelings follow. Consider this for a moment: if you concentrate on everything you want to avoid in life, you will likely experience more negativity, and your brain will unconsciously seek out those negative aspects. As you begin to shift your mindset and incorporate brain science tools to improve your life, you'll notice a greater influx of positive experiences. You'll find yourself engaging in more intentional actions that generate even more goodness, leading to an uplifting cycle where you begin to feel increasingly better.

However, it's crucial to remember that it's not just about the actions you take; you must also focus on capturing the feelings associated with what you truly desire. If you solely concentrate on the doing, you may find yourself in a perpetual chase for feelings that come only after achieving your goals. I encourage you to connect with how you want to feel and to cultivate those emotions regularly. When you prioritize experiencing those feelings, the things you desire will come to you more effortlessly. A great tool for this is to think of at least three times in your life when you experienced immense joy. Really go back and remember the feelings you had with it, then go through each one of those three when you're feeling really great, then take that feeling and think about achieving the new goal, adding these same incredible feelings.

It's important to be mindful that longing for something can create a barrier; the absence of what you want can evoke sadness or lower emotional frequencies. While having goals is valuable, try to concentrate on elevating your emotions in a more positive way. I greatly admire Deb Dana's work with her emotional ladder, which illustrates how to navigate emotional states. Even before I learned about her ladder, I encouraged my clients to develop a personal toolbox filled with strategies to elevate their mood. This toolbox serves as a resource when you find yourself in a challenging emotional place.

Deb Dana beautifully describes how being at the lower rungs of the emotional ladder, such as feeling frozen or depressed, can make it difficult to envision or reach the heights of joy and excitement. Yet, like climbing a ladder, you can take small steps upward. Each step toward feeling even slightly better can lead to the next, gradually lifting your emotional state. As you ascend, you might experience feelings of anxiety or anger, which, while not ideal, can be more productive than feeling immobilized or depressed. It is essential to recognize that moving up the ladder, even incrementally, is a step in the right direction.

To advance, ask yourself, "What can I do to elevate my emotional state one step higher or at this time?" Utilizing the tools we have discussed, and others we will explore, allows you to give yourself permission to ascend without judgment or frustration. Acknowledging what helps you climb the ladder is the first step; jotting down these strategies ensures you have a plan when you feel stuck. Over time, you'll find that you can maintain a higher emotional state more consistently.

It's vital to remember that when your brain is in a state of fight, flight, or freeze, it can be easy to forget the tools that can help you climb the emotional ladder. Therefore, having a written toolbox of strategies that resonate with you can provide peace and clarity during challenging times. Consider keeping this toolbox on your phone or in a place at home where you can easily access it. Knowing you have these resources can empower you to navigate your emotions more effectively.

I also believe the ladder is helpful because being in a state that is depression and trying to jump to excitement may be too far-reaching and make you feel the movement is impossible. When going from depressed to excited can be very difficult, however, you could go from depressed to feeling at ease, and that would be moving up the ladder.

Here are a few of my favorites:

1. **Music:** Music is a powerful source of vibrations, so take a moment to close your eyes and immerse yourself in the feelings and images that the songs you choose evoke. I have created several playlists for different purposes: one for inspiration, another for cleaning, one for focus and concentration, and one to uplift my mornings. You can create as many as you like!

   Nearly three decades ago, my licensed supervisor imparted a valuable lesson during my internship: It's essential to find ways to leave work behind and transition to home life, especially in a field that can easily lead to burnout. She didn't prescribe a specific solution, but what came to me was the idea of using music. Every day, I would pop a cassette (yes, a cassette... Time flies!) into my car music player and listen to it on my drive home. This simple act felt liberating, as if I were releasing my day's burdens and entrusting them to God, creating a peaceful atmosphere for my commute.

This practice not only transformed my own experience but also became a tool I used with my clients over the years. Many of them held high-stress jobs: police officers, doctors, lawyers, counselors, coaches, military personnel, EMTs, nurses, and firefighters. Together, we would craft personalized playlists that they could listen to on their way home, facilitating a neuro transition that allowed them to leave work behind and reconnect with their home life.

This approach proved especially beneficial for those in hyper-vigilant roles, as they often struggled to shake off the intense energy of their jobs. Rather than bringing this heightened state home, they would frequently shut down emotionally or become irritable, leaving their families to feel the impact. I explained to them and their loved ones that their brains were attempting to protect their families by not sharing the day's burdens. They often didn't realize they were bringing home the emotional weight of their experiences, making it challenging to reconnect with their loved ones.

As healing progressed, clients would express how incredible it felt to metaphorically remove their work persona like a hat or coat the moment they entered their car. This simple yet profound practice allowed them to transition back into their home life with renewed energy and presence.

2. **Affirmations:** Sometimes I say a list of affirmations, and other times I listen to affirmations. I have a few playlists I saved, like Louis Hayes,

Bob Proctor, Michael Beckwith, and others. Remember, listening to words can transform our state because words, even heard, elicit a chemical response in the brain and body.

3. **Movement:** Negative energy and stress can become trapped in our bodies, leaving us feeling weighed down mentally, physically, and emotionally. Recent research has shed light on how our bodies store stress responses and even traumatic experiences. However, movement serves as a powerful antidote, helping us to release some of that stagnant energy. I personally enjoy practices like Tai Chi, Qi Gong, gentle stretches throughout the day, or simply dancing to shake off tension.

In the past, I gravitated toward high-impact activities such as aerobics, karate aerobics, running, and Zumba, which were all exhilarating. However, after facing health challenges due to an autoimmune condition that arose from not allowing my body sufficient rest, I transitioned to gentler forms of movement. Surprisingly, I discovered that these softer exercises were not only effective for stress relief but also much kinder to my body. One of my favorite easy practices for those who have severe health issues or who have very little time is Lee Holden's "7 Minutes of Magic" Qi Gong routine. You can find it on YouTube.

For those of you who may have neurodivergent conditions like ADHD, you might relate to my initial experience with Tai Chi and Qi Gong. At first, it felt akin to learning to deal with a resistant, awkward, and challenging feeling because I was accustomed to a fast-paced lifestyle. I thrived on speed and productivity throughout my day. Yet, through my journey of illness, I realized that slowing down and engaging in these more relaxed forms of exercise introduced a positive energy within me, contrasting sharply with the negative energy that had been contributing to my condition.

If you are dealing with any debilitating illness, you might find that there are chair-based movements available, including adaptations of Tai Chi and Qi Gong. These gentle practices can provide an accessible way to harness the benefits of movement while respecting your body's needs.

4. **Laughter:** Curate videos that make you laugh until your sides ache. Laughter enhances health and well-being; even fake laughter stimulates the release of positive chemicals and can even bring healing to cells.

   Research shows that laughter lowers stress hormones, reduces anxiety, and boosts the immune system. It improves circulation and cardiovascular health, acting as a natural workout for your heart.

   Laughter also strengthens social bonds, creates memories, and boosts mental clarity and creativity. Incorporating laughter into your routine—through funny videos, stand-up comedy shows, or sharing stories—can brighten your days and elevate your health. Embrace this joyous gift!

5. **Instruments:** Playing music on a guitar, drums, gong, or any other instrument, and feeling into it as you breathe out can be helpful. Even beating on the drums or singing has proven to be very beneficial for individuals to release stress from the body. More recent research has continued to explore the impact of music and singing on the body. A study published in 2021 in the journal *Frontiers in Psychology* highlights that singing can significantly reduce cortisol levels, the hormone associated with stress, and reduce pain in the body, leading to improved mental health. The study highlights several review articles: one, which focused on group singing, not only enhancing mood but also strengthening immune response, showcasing the physiological benefits of musical engagement. These findings underscore the idea that music acts as a powerful tool for healing, promoting not just emotional well-being but also physical health. By

engaging in singing, we harness the ability to foster resilience in our bodies and minds, offering a natural and enjoyable avenue for stress relief and emotional connection.

6. **Aromatherapy:** Keep a selection of scents on hand, such as peppermint, lavender, eucalyptus, or orange...whichever fragrances help you feel more centered and grounded. A simple yet effective technique is to place a few drops of peppermint oil on your hands, rub them together, and then bring your hands to your nose, breathing in deeply. This calming practice is not only beneficial for adults but can also be soothing for children. Remember, children have a higher sense of sensitivity, so be mindful when using it with children.

If you are particularly sensitive to scents, start with just a small drop or avoid applying it too close to your face. Alternatively, you can place a drop on a small piece of cloth to keep near your workspace or use a diffuser to disperse the aroma throughout your environment. This can create a more pleasant atmosphere and promote easier breathing, enhancing your overall sense of well-being. There are some great research articles on using aromatherapy even in hospitals with great success.

7. **Taste:** Peppermint or spearmint candies, like Tic Tacs or menthols, or Lifesavers can be wonderful for grounding. As you pop one into your mouth, focus on your breathing. Instead of chewing, let it dissolve slowly while you inhale and exhale, noticing how this simple act brings a sense of calm. This technique is especially useful for those who experience anxiety while driving or struggle with road rage, as it encourages you to slow down and reconnect with a more tranquil state of mind. Working with combat veterans and first responders, many with PTSD, who struggled with road rage, this was very helpful for them. I recall one time when a veteran said, "Hey, my wife said you said peppermints would help my road rage, and I will have you know I ate ten on the way here and it didn't help at all." I said did you suck

on them or chew them. You see chewing them puts tension in the jaw but sucking on them helps you to breathe more. The next time I saw him, he said it actually helped a lot. Additionally, savoring a warm cup of cocoa or flavored tea can provide comfort and serenity, making it a delightful way to enhance your well-being.

8. **Combination of These:** You can do a combination of tools to move up the ladder. If one thing doesn't work, try something else until you feel a release and more peace and joy. Sometimes, we get in our own way when something doesn't work, and forget that each tool creates different responses in the brain and body. You're not a failure; you're not doing it all wrong. Sometimes, it takes more effort than others. Tune in and pray and ask yourself, "What might work better?" Remember, "You are the artist of your life, paint the life you want with God as your Compass" (Erica Elliott).

Take a moment to write your own uplifting reset toolbox down:

_____

_____

_____

_____

_____

_____

_____

_____

_____

_____

Conclusion

Harnessing the power of your mind is essential for effective manifestation. By utilizing tools such as neuroplasticity, mindfulness meditation, gratitude practices, positive affirmations, and visualization techniques, you can align your brain's functions with your goals and desires. Creating and using vision boards can significantly enhance your manifestation abilities by keeping your aspirations vividly present and reinforcing your commitment to them.

Incorporating these methods into your daily routine will strengthen your capacity to bring your desires to fruition. Embrace the strength of your mind, guided by your brain's wisdom and your spirit's connection to a higher power. When your thoughts, beliefs, and actions align, you'll create a life that resonates with your deepest aspirations. The journey of manifestation is both a mental and spiritual experience. By applying these practical techniques, you are well on your way to realizing your dreams and fulfilling your divine potential and purpose.

"You Are the Artist of Your Life, Paint the Life You Want with God as Your Compass,"
—Erica Elliott.

Reflection Notes

CHAPTER 8

Overcoming Doubts and Negative Thoughts

Doubts and negative thoughts present significant challenges on the path to manifestation. They erode our confidence, create obstacles to success, and disrupt the positive energy flow necessary for achieving our goals. Additionally, they can hinder our ability to connect with divine guidance and listen to our inner wisdom. Overcoming these mental barriers requires us to identify and confront limiting beliefs, utilize biblical strategies to counteract doubt and negativity, and apply psychological techniques to foster a positive mindset. This chapter will delve into these elements, offering you a thorough approach to cultivating a resilient and optimistic outlook.

Throughout my life, I have grappled with negative thoughts and beliefs, but I have learned to transform them over the years using various tools and techniques. Our beliefs often stem from diverse sources—our upbringing, the people around us, school, church, and workplaces. I resonate with the idea that beliefs are merely thoughts we keep thinking until they solidify into something we accept as true. Reflecting on my childhood, I now recognize that I displayed signs of ADHD, even though it wasn't diagnosed in the 1980s, especially in girls. I struggled significantly with negative thoughts, but I eventually discovered tools to combat them. My initial approach was rooted in perfectionism; I believed that achieving excellence would earn me approval and validation. While accolades made me feel good temporarily, they also reinforced the belief that my worth depended on my accomplishments.

I would chase perfection, but when I inevitably fell short, frustration and disappointment would set in. This cycle led to tears and self-doubt. I also realized that I lacked positive role models; those around me often celebrated workaholism. To illustrate, during my senior year of high school, I juggled five jobs including being a preschool teacher, managing a retail outlet, cashier for grocery store, participating in a delayed entry program for the military on the weekends, and when I wasn't doing all of that, I helped my mom paint and set up for arts and craft shows. I knew I wanted a different future and sought a college education, which motivated me to join the military for financial assistance.

As a young person, I immersed myself in exploring my faith and spending time in the Bible, searching for clarity about my path. While I occasionally felt a strong sense of direction, I often found myself distracted by external pressures and negative self-talk that clouded my understanding of what truly nourished my spirit. The tools I will share in the following sections are ones I have personally cultivated and continue to revisit. I also teach these techniques to others because they are genuinely transformative. To create the life we desire, we must shift our beliefs and reprogram our minds, paving the way for growth and fulfillment. Remember God's Word says to take every (not just some) thought captive to make it obedient to Christ. 2 Corinthians 10:5 (NIV): "*We demolish arguments and every pretension that sets itself up against the knowledge of God, and we take every thought captive to make it obedient to Christ.*" Meaning if our thoughts don't align with what God's word says about us, our circumstances and others we change those thoughts to reflect God's Word - God's Promises. In Christ we are a new creation and old things are passed away - we have become new. (2 Corinthians 5:17 KJV)

Identifying and Challenging Limiting Beliefs

Limiting beliefs are the deep-seated thoughts and convictions that restrict our potential. They often stem from past experiences, common societal conditioning, and internalized negative feedback. Identifying these beliefs is the first step towards overcoming them.

1. **Self-Reflection:** Spend time reflecting on your thoughts and feelings. Pay attention to recurring negative thoughts or statements you make about yourself. For instance, if you frequently think, "I'm not good

enough," "I always fail, mess up," "I'm not trying hard enough," or "Something is wrong with me," these are indications of limiting beliefs.

2. **Journaling:** Keep a journal to document your thoughts, especially those related to your goals and abilities. Writing down your thoughts can help you identify patterns and pinpoint specific limiting beliefs.

3. **Feedback from Others:** Sometimes, others can see our limiting beliefs more clearly than we can. Seek feedback from trusted friends or mentors who can provide an objective perspective.

4. **Mindfulness:** Practice mindfulness to become more aware of your thought patterns. Mindfulness involves observing your thoughts without judgment, which can help you recognize limiting beliefs as they arise.

Challenging Limiting Beliefs

Once you have identified your limiting beliefs, the next step is to challenge and replace them with empowering thoughts.

1. **Question the Evidence:** Analyze the evidence supporting your limiting beliefs. Ask yourself, "Is this belief based on facts or assumptions?" Often, you will find these beliefs are NOT grounded in reality.

2. **Dive Deeper:** Ask yourself, "Who said..." (insert limiting belief). Reflect on whether or not you remember anyone in your family or someone you were around a lot who said those same kinds of things. Whose voice is it really?

3. **What Does God's Word Say:** Look up scripture references around this area. Many times, we realize God wants so much good for us, and His Word proves these limiting beliefs wrong.

4. **Reframe Negative Thoughts:** Reframe your negative thoughts into positive statements. For example, replace "I can't do this" with "I am

learning and improving every day." Plus, God's Word says, "I can do all things through Christ who strengthens me" (Philippians 4:13). This shift in mindset helps cultivate self-esteem and opens the door to growth and resilience.

5. **Gather Counter-Evidence:** Collect evidence that contradicts your limiting beliefs. Reflect on past successes and times when you have overcome challenges. Use these examples to build a case against your limiting beliefs.

6. **Affirmations:** Create positive affirmations that counteract your limiting beliefs. Repeat these affirmations daily to reinforce new neural connections and empowering beliefs. For instance, if you struggle with self-doubt, state and affirm that "I am capable and confident and getting better every day."

7. **Visualization:** Visualize yourself succeeding and achieving your goals. This mental imagery can help you shift your mindset and reinforce your new, positive beliefs.

Biblical Strategies for Combating Doubt and Negativity

The Bible offers numerous strategies for overcoming doubt and negativity. By grounding yourself and biblical truth, you can strengthen your faith and maintain a positive outlook.

1. **Prayer:** Prayer is a powerful tool for combating doubt and negativity. Philippians 4:6-7 encourages us to present our requests to God through prayer and thanksgiving, promising that His peace will guard our hearts and minds. Regular prayer helps us release our worries to God and trust in His plan.

2. **Scripture Memorization:** Memorizing scriptures that address doubt and negativity can provide a source of comfort and strength. Verses like Isaiah 41:10, "So do not fear, or I am with you; do not be

dismayed, for I am your God," remind us of God's constant presence and support.

3. **Worship and Praise:** Engaging in worship and praise can lift our spirits and shift our focus from our problems to God's greatness. Singing hymns, listening to worship music, and expressing gratitude can dispel negative thoughts and bring joy. Not to mention how wonderful music brings in wonderful positive chemicals into our body and brain.

4. **Fellowship with Believers:** Surrounding yourself with a supportive community of believers can help you stay positive and encouraged. Hebrews 10:24-25 emphasizes the importance of encouraging one another and meeting together regularly.

5. **Biblical Meditation:** Meditating on God's Word involves deeply reflecting on scriptures and applying them to your life. Joshua 1:8 advises meditating on the Word day and night to ensure prosperity and success. This practice helps align your thoughts with God's promises to strengthen your faith. This is a tool that can help us every day, and especially when we're feeling stuck.

6. **Casting Your Cares on God:** 1 Peter 5:7 reminds us to "cast all our anxiety on God because he cares for us." Remember that He says ALL, not some of our cares. This act of surrender helps alleviate the burden of doubt and negativity, allowing us to trust in God's provision and care.

Psychological Techniques for Maintaining a Positive Mindset

In addition to biblical strategies, psychological techniques can effectively combat doubt and negativity and help maintain a positive mindset.

1. **Cognitive Behavioral Therapy (CBT):** CBT is a therapeutic approach that focuses on changing negative thought patterns and

behaviors. By identifying and challenging cognitive distortions, you can develop healthier thinking habits. Techniques such as thought records, where you document and analyze negative thoughts, can be particularly helpful. There are a lot of great apps for CBT as well.

2. **Mindfulness and Meditation:** Cultivating mindfulness and meditation can significantly enhance our awareness and acceptance of thoughts and emotions. Techniques such as deep breathing and body scans are effective in reducing stress and enhancing mental clarity. Regular meditation practice has been shown to foster positive emotions while diminishing negative thinking. It's important to recognize that everyone experiences a wide range of thoughts and feelings. When we learn to observe them without judgment and let them go, we gain greater control over the thoughts that truly serve us.

   Research indicates that the average person has between 60,000 and 80,000 thoughts each day, with approximately 70% of those being negative or critical. This tendency is not a reflection of your worth; rather, it's a common pattern within our minds. However, we have the power to release or redirect our focus away from thoughts that do not contribute to our well-being. By practicing mindfulness, we can cultivate a more positive mindset and embrace the thoughts that uplift and empower us.

3. **Gratitude Practice:** Emphasizing gratitude can profoundly uplift your mood and perspective. Consider keeping a gratitude journal where you jot down at least five things you appreciate each day, along with any other positive experiences you encounter. This practice of reflecting on the bright moments in your life can help shift your attention away from negativity and nurture a sense of contentment. On tougher days, revisiting your journal can be especially beneficial. It serves as a reminder of times when things were going well, helping to elevate your spirits and reinforce your faith in brighter days ahead. By consistently acknowledging the good, you cultivate a mindset that

embraces positivity and resilience. It's interesting and inspiring that there are people who have completely changed their whole lives just by implementing gratitude in their lives.

4. **Positive Visualization:** Visualizing positive outcomes and success can boost your confidence and motivation. Spend time each day visualizing yourself achieving your goals and experiencing the emotions associated with that success. This practice can help you reinforce positive thinking and keep you focused on your desired outcomes. You can also visualize the good things that happened the day before or days before that will help bring up positive outcome thoughts.

5. **Self-Compassion:** Treat yourself with kindness and understanding, especially during difficult times. Self-compassion involves recognizing that everyone makes mistakes and experiences setbacks. Instead of criticizing yourself, offer yourself words of encouragement and support, much like you would to a friend or someone you were teaching.

6. **Exercise and Physical Activity:** Regular physical activity has been shown to improve mood and reduce symptoms of anxiety and depression. Exercise releases endorphins, which are natural mood lifters. Find an activity you enjoy and make it a regular part of your routine.

7. **Healthy Lifestyle Choices:** Maintaining a healthy lifestyle can support your mental well-being. Ensure you get enough sleep, eat a balanced diet, and stay hydrated. Avoid substances that can negatively impact your mood, such as excessive caffeine and alcohol.

8. **Setting Realistic Goals:** Establishing and accomplishing small, achievable goals can greatly enhance your self-esteem and create a feeling of success. By deconstructing larger objectives into smaller, more manageable tasks, you can celebrate each milestone, which in turn helps you remain motivated and fosters a positive mindset.

I like to compare the process of rewiring your brain to the rehabilitation of someone recovering from a brain injury. Just as it may take numerous attempts to regain skills lost due to an injury, reshaping deeply rooted mental habits also demands time and effort. These entrenched behaviors have often existed for many years, so it's crucial to take a similar approach. Expect it to take a while for your new behaviors to become instinctive. Remember, you are not just eliminating detrimental patterns but also developing new, constructive habits that will transform your mindset for the better.

Conclusion

Conquering doubts and negative thoughts is essential for effective manifestation. By recognizing and confronting limiting beliefs, applying biblical principles, and embracing psychological strategies, you can cultivate a positive mindset that keeps you aligned with your aspirations. Keep in mind that this journey demands ongoing effort and dedication, but the benefits are truly transformative.

As you weave these strategies into your everyday routine, you will discover that you are more equipped to face challenges, sustain your faith, and bring your deepest desires to fruition in harmony with God's purpose. This process not only strengthens your resolve but also deepens your connection to your true path.

Psychological Techniques for Maintaining a Positive Mindset

Interactive Questions and Exercises

Cognitive Behavioral Techniques

Exercise: Identify a negative thought you frequently have. Use the CBT technique of thought challenging by asking yourself the following questions:

1. What evidence supports this thought?

_____

_____

2. What evidence contradicts this thought?

_____

_____

_____

3. Who in my life says things like this? (Sometimes, the inner critic is tied to a parental figure, boss, teacher, or mate.)

_____

_____

_____

4. What would I say to a friend who has this thought?

_____

_____

_____

5. What is a more balanced or realistic way of thinking about this situation? Write down your answers and reflect on how this process helps. You will see the thought in a new light.

_____

_____

_____

Creating a Support System

Cultivating a positive support network can be immensely helpful as you strive to shift behaviors and habits in your life. There is a well-known saying that we tend to mirror the three to five people we spend the most time with. Therefore, as you build your support system, focus on surrounding yourself with individuals who are also dedicated to personal development, positivity, and mutual encouragement.

Although creating a supportive environment can sometimes pose challenges, exploring options like hiring a coach or engaging in group coaching can be advantageous. This allows you to connect with others who share similar goals, offering you both companionship and inspiration as you navigate your journey together. Being in the company of like-minded individuals can enhance your progress and make the transformative experience more fulfilling.

Exercise: Identify three people in your life who provide positive support and encouragement. Reach out to them and share your goals and challenges. Ask for their support and accountability. Reflect on how having a support system helps you stay positive and motivated.

_____

_____

_____

_____

Conclusion

Conquering doubts and negative thoughts is essential for effective manifestation. By recognizing and questioning limiting beliefs, applying biblical principles, and incorporating psychological techniques, you can foster a positive mindset that keeps you in harmony with your goals. It's important to remember that this journey requires ongoing effort and practice, but the rewards are truly remarkable.

As you weave these strategies into your everyday life, you'll find yourself more capable of facing challenges, sustaining your faith, and bringing your deepest desires to life in alignment with God's purpose. To enhance your understanding and application of these principles, take advantage of the interactive questions and exercises included in this chapter. They will guide you in transforming your thoughts and beliefs, ultimately reshaping your reality. Remember, "You have the power to change your environment by your attitude, your smile, your language, your tone, your energy. It's all inside of you" (Erica Elliott).

"You Have the Power to Change Your Environment by Your Attitude, Your Smile, Your Language, Your Tone, Your Energy ~ It's All Inside of You," —Erica Elliott

Reflection Notes

CHAPTER 9

Blocks to Blessings

In the previous chapter, we looked at limiting beliefs, which can be a huge block to blessings. However, there are other obstacles that can block the flow of blessings in your life. Let's review some of these, so you can create a life that is more aligned with a successful, abundantly blessed life.

Financial Blocks

The Bible is really clear on many things regarding money. It is one of the few areas that God actually says to try him in this and see if he will not pour out blessings upon you. "'Bring the whole tithe into the storehouse, that there may be food in my house. Test me in this,' says the Lord Almighty, 'and see if I will not throw open the floodgates of heaven and pour out so much blessing that there will not be room enough to store it.'" (Malachi 3:10)

Throughout my journey, I have encountered numerous individuals, both within and outside the church community, who wholeheartedly embrace the concept of sowing and reaping—the belief that what you give will ultimately return to you above what you can imagine. A significant barrier many face is a scarcity mindset, which often hinders financial flow into our lives. I frequently remind those who feel unable to contribute 10% of their earnings to a worthy cause to reflect on whether this mindset might be obstructing their blessings.

I vividly remember many occasions in church where business owners made contributions even if they weren't regular attendees, simply because they recognized that their generosity led to abundant blessings for themselves and their businesses. While they might not have fully understood the mechanics, they knew that withholding their support often resulted in a lack of prosperity.

When I work with individuals who express that they cannot afford to give, we explore alternative avenues for contribution.

My deep understanding of this concept began to evolve in my mid-twenties. I've always been someone who seeks knowledge, diving into research to comprehend how things function. Thus, when it came to finances, I was bewildered by the fact that despite receiving raises, I continually found myself in debt. Having witnessed God's principles come to life in various aspects of my existence, I decided to dive deeper into the Bible and learn from experts in financial management through literature. The psychological side of me recognized that to truly grasp a subject, one must study it thoroughly, especially from those who have mastered it. One book that profoundly impacted me was *Rags to Riches* by Tom Leading, with a foreword by Pat Robertson. Although I had read many texts, this concise guide offered actionable steps for improving one's financial circumstances, igniting a desire within me to implement some of its strategies.

One pivotal lesson was to tithe based on my gross income instead of my net. I distinctly remember trying to explain this to my then-husband, emphasizing the importance of giving from our gross income, even with our existing debt. He thought I was irrational, which led to a heated discussion. However, deep within, I felt this was a crucial truth. Even while juggling two jobs, I decided to move forward with tithing from my income, regardless of his perspective. I also committed to seeking God's wisdom on how to manage my finances more effectively.

Allowing God to influence my financial decisions opened my eyes in unexpected ways. I recall anticipating birthday money, having prayed for guidance on how to use it wisely. I had my heart set on acquiring two stunning suits from Chadwick's, a store known for quality attire but also affordable prices. When a catalog arrived offering an incredible deal—two suits for $39—I felt elated. However, I wanted to ensure that this was the right choice for my birthday funds.

When I sought God's guidance regarding this purchase, I felt a profound sense of reluctance; it was as if I were Cinderella and God was the stern stepmother. The answer I received was not what I expected: I was to give the money away to bless someone else. Accepting this directive was not easy; while I wanted to grow in my ability to heed God's voice, I also felt a genuine need for those suits. I couldn't claim that I gave that money away happily at first; in fact, it felt somewhat heartbreaking, akin to being punished. Yet, I remembered the scripture that encourages us to give cheerfully, prompting me to express gratitude for the many blessings in my life. With that shift in attitude, I surrendered the money to God, trusting Him to guide its use.

The very next day, my husband mentioned a young woman from another country who had become pregnant and was struggling without support from her family. She attended the same university I had graduated from, and I immediately felt a strong urge to help her. I took her shopping for essentials, and as we connected, I was reminded of the profound joy that comes from uplifting others in need.

This experience reaffirmed that when we give to those who are struggling, we not only bless them but also enrich our own lives in unexpected ways. Shortly afterward, I came across a garage sale on my way home. Despite being cautious with my spending, I felt a compelling urge to stop. What transpired was nothing short of miraculous. I discovered several high-quality suits in my favorite color, still with tags, priced at just five dollars each. One of those suits had a retail tag indicating a price of $189, and they were all my size!

Do you believe in miracles? Do you believe that God desires good things for you? I left that garage sale in awe, having spent approximately $20 on four brand-new suits. A family member even gifted me another suit for my birthday. I was in disbelief—was this a dream, or merely a coincidence? I was eager to see what further blessings awaited me, so I began seeking God's guidance on how to allocate my income, including my tithe.

There have been countless moments where God prompted me to give my last dollar or five-dollar bill meant for a meal, leading to incredible financial blessings in return—often multiple times what I had given. I had asked God to teach me to trust Him with my finances, and He was certainly delivering those lessons.

As I continued to experience these blessings, my enthusiasm for tithing on my gross income grew. However, this commitment didn't yield immediate results, which made me feel somewhat anxious. I turned to prayer and worship, claiming God's promise that if I gave, He would return it pressed down, shaken together, and overflowing. By the second month of my tithing journey, I prayed for a swing set and not only received one free ($350 value) but two—my parents took the second one for their home. Eventually, my husband became more receptive to the idea of tithing and, by the third or fourth month, we found ourselves relieved of $20,000 in debt. We also received a brand-new recliner that perfectly complemented our living room and had a built-in massage feature. I was utterly astonished! We desperately needed a new recliner, ours was threadbare and looked awful, plus sunk in. How awesome God is!!! He not only meets our needs but also our wants many times, too.

As I practiced generosity, I realized that I could NOT outgive God. By the sixth month, I had received two raises, which was unprecedented at my workplace, along with a bonus. My heart swelled with gratitude—thank you, God! Your Word is indeed true! You do want good for our lives!

I've heard individuals express a desire to adopt these principles, only to insist they simply cannot at this moment or that their partner opposes it. Over the years, I've encouraged many to search their homes for items they could donate to bless others. I can't tell you how often people return, sharing that once they gave, financial blessings began to flow into their lives.

One particular story stands out: a woman shared her struggles after her husband lost his job. Despite their financial difficulties, they recognized the importance of tithing, yet her husband was hesitant. They decided to gather items from their home to donate, praying for guidance on what to give away. Shortly thereafter, they began to experience financial blessings, and her husband secured a new job. They were astonished at how quickly their situation improved, unsure how they could ever repay their tithes. I encouraged them to seek God's forgiveness and start anew, much like the Prodigal Son. God does not wish to burden us; He loves us and desires to show us the abundant life we can experience when we follow His guidance. Be careful not to fall into the thought that if you turn to God, he's going to make you pay for denying him in the past. That's not God! He loves you and wants you to succeed in life.

It's important to note that you don't have to be a Christian for the law of sowing and reaping to take effect—what you sow, you shall reap. The Bible teaches that if you sow sparingly, you will reap sparingly, but if you sow generously, you will reap abundantly. Many individuals from various faith backgrounds, including those who do not believe in God, testify that their generosity has brought them blessings. These principles are universal, transcending religious boundaries and proving that generosity can lead to remarkable outcomes for anyone willing to embrace it.

A few steps to remember:

1. **Pray and Ask God Where to Tithe Your 10%:** If you want more blessings, tithe on your gross. I remember hearing of someone who got so good at this that they began tithing 90%, and the money was so abundant that they would never be able to spend it in a lifetime.

2. **Give Things That Equal Money:** Go around your house and find things you can give, and ask God to direct you in who or where you need to give it to.

3. **Give Time:** Money is equivalent to time, and time is equivalent to money, so if you absolutely don't see where you could give money, ask where you could give your time.

4. **Give Joyfully:** Get in a joyful spirit when you give. Put on some worship music if you need to.

5. **Speaking God's Word Over Your Giving:** "Father God, you said if I would give, you would give back, press down shaken together and running over!" There is power in speaking His Word.

6. **Believe:** Believe that God will fulfill His promises. I love the analogy God shows us to have the faith the size of a mustard seed. Could you consider the possibility that God may want to bless your life plus show others His love through you?

Read and Meditate on Scriptures About Money

Here are a few scriptures to get you started:

"Give and it shall be given unto you. A good measure, pressed down, shaken together, and running over, will be poured into your lap. For with the measure you use, it will be measured to you." (Luke 6:38)

"A generous person will prosper; whoever refreshes others will be refreshed." (Psalms 11:25)

"Remember this: whoever sows sparingly will also reap sparingly, and whoever sows generously will also reap generously." (2 Corinthians 9:6)

"The blessing of the Lord brings wealth, without painful toil for it." (Proverbs 10:22)

"And my God will meet all your needs according to the riches of his glory in Christ Jesus." (Philippians 4:19)

"There is treasure to be desired and oil in the dwelling of the wise; but a foolish man spendeth it up." (Proverbs 21:20)

"Then he said to them, watch out! Be on your guard against all kinds of greed; life does not consist in abundance of possessions." (Luke 12:15)

"No one can serve two masters. Either you will hate the one and love the other, or you will be devoted to the one and despise the other. You cannot serve both God and money." (Matthew 6:24)

Speaking Curses

The teachings of the Bible emphasize the importance of being mindful of our words. Our speech can bring forth both blessings and curses. It's possible that we may be hindering our own blessings through the words we choose to express.

This is an area where I have had to put in significant effort. I recall grappling with whether or not voicing my true feelings was a form of dishonesty. Even now, I find it essential to pause and consider whether what I'm about to say aligns with my intentions, beliefs, and faith. Growing up in an environment where words were often carelessly thrown around made learning to control my tongue a challenge. However, one of the most rewarding skills you can cultivate is the ability to tame your tongue. Interestingly, science suggests that when we say things like "I don't want" something, our brains interpret that as a desire for it. This goes beyond mere positive thinking—this is about wielding the power of your words to work in your favor. Remember to practice speaking what you want, not what you don't want.

I liken this to the wisdom of Master Yoda, who often chose silence over unnecessary words, conveying profound truths in just a few syllables. The Bible makes it clear that our words hold immense power: "The tongue has the power of life and death, and those who love it will eat its fruits" (Proverbs 18:21). What does this even mean? It means whatever you are speaking affirmatively, which is faith, is speaking as if it's true and not mailable. So, if you are dealing with something that is true, like struggling in a particular area, it would be better for you to say I am working on getting better in this particular area than to say I have this where I end this, or that's just the way that I am. Coming up, I will share how to understand and shift your words. Another verse reminds us that "Whoever keeps their mouth and their tongue keeps themselves from troubles" (Proverbs 21:23). Some refer to this practice as making declarations—asserting what you want to manifest in your life.

In my work in trauma counseling, I often hear the belief that discussing painful experiences is essential until the negative emotions subside. While sharing your story is indeed valuable, it's crucial to consider how repetition affects the brain and body. Each time you recount your narrative, you reinforce those neural connections. It's important to reflect on whether you are sharing your story to release it and move forward, or whether you are stuck replaying it in your mind and creating more triggers as if this is now who you are. If it's the latter, you may want to seek guidance from a qualified mental health professional who can help you process and defuse the triggers associated with your experiences, allowing you to live more fully in the present and build the life you desire.

I want to emphasize that I'm not minimizing the reality of trauma, or the challenges posed by PTSD or complex PTSD. Healing takes time and dedicated effort, and I highly recommend finding a skilled mental health professional experienced in trauma-informed practices such as EMDR and somatic therapy. It's also important to clarify that I'm not suggesting silence or that the Word of God advocates for never speaking how we feel. Instead, it encourages us to be aware of our words, as they yield either fruitful outcomes or unwelcome weeds. Jesus even exhibited lots of different emotions. Let yourself feel an emotion and you can even say I allow myself to feel stress even though I don't want to feel stress as a way to release this out of the body as you will find in an exercise I share here in the book. It's also absolutely okay and can be very helpful when speaking to someone identifying a feeling you have - like say, I felt hurt when you did.... However, using declarations in our speech is where we really want to pay attention. What are you declaring as you speak? Declaring is a testimony like proclaiming. Think to yourself, if God's word says for us to declare or proclaim what we want are some of our declarations out of alignment. Remember we can't change what we don't notice.

James 3:4-5 (NIV): "Or take ships as an example. Although they are so large and are driven by strong winds, they are steered by a very small rudder wherever the pilot wants to go. Likewise, the tongue is a small part of the body, but it makes great boasts. Consider what a great forest is set on fire by a small spark!" This passage illustrates the power of the tongue and how it can influence our actions and direction in life.

Some people may say, well you want to tell the truth don't you. Hmm...Is it the truth based on the Word of God or a belief we have allowed to come in like a weed? These things aren't meant to create us condemning our life but to be observant for creating our life with God's Word as our declaration. As we are changing our life we have to get honest with ourselves, and that means cleaning up some of the mess that hinders us being the Masterpiece Manifestor God has given us the right to be.

I continue to work on this aspect of my life. Years ago, I read Joyce Meyer's book *Me and My Big Mouth*. I wholeheartedly encourage anyone struggling with the words you flow from your mouth to explore it. It's filled with wisdom and practical tips for mastering the art of communication in a way that focuses on what we want and controlling our tongue.

The Bible also advises against judgment, reminding us that when we judge others, we are not only sending out negativity but also inviting it back into our own lives. There's a saying that when you point a finger at someone else, four fingers are pointing back at you. It's nearly impossible to fully comprehend another person's experiences unless you've walked in their shoes or lived within their thoughts. Therefore, it's wise to recognize that the judgments we cast upon others may very well return to us, often as negative consequences. Let's break down how our speech could hinder versus create more health.

Here are a few examples:

Commands Toward Negative	Commands Toward Positive	Commands to Rewire New Beliefs
I hate driving.	The traffic is busy today, but it's not always this busy.	I am learning to enjoy driving, knowing God is always taking care of me.
I am always sick.	I feel sick right now, but I know I will get better. Or I don't feel well right now, but every day I believe God will help me get better and better.	Even though I don't feel good, I'm so grateful for my body and I know by Christ stripes I am healing and getting better and better.
I am always late.	I am running late right now, but I usually do very well with time.	I am running late right now, but I know I will settle back into a good pace.
I'm never going to get this right.	I didn't get it right this time, but sometimes I do.	I may not have gotten it right this time, but if I keep practicing, I will get better and better.

Practice: Make a list of words you often say and rewrite them.

Commands Toward Negative	Commands Toward Positive	Commands to Rewire New Beliefs

Generational Curses

We live in an era where discussions about genetics and inherited traits are commonplace. How often have you been asked by a doctor if any family members have experienced certain health issues? If our words wield such power, consider the implications of saying things like, "I'll probably have that because a family member did." Plus, many doctors will say, "Well, if your parents had it, you probably will, too." This reinforces the importance of being mindful of our language. However, it's equally vital to recognize that we have the authority to break these cycles of negativity, as God's Word assures us.

Let's explore some scripture concerning generational curses. For instance, "The Lord is slow to anger, abounding in love and forgiving sin and rebellion. Yet he does not leave the guilty unpunished; he punishes the children for the sin of the parents to the third generation" (Numbers 14:18). This raises the question: What exactly is sin? According to 1 John 3:4, "Everyone who sins breaks the law; in fact, sin is lawlessness." This understanding reveals that we all fall short, as we've all broken God's laws.

Another significant verse regarding curses is found in Exodus 20:5: "You shall not bow down to them or worship them; for I, the Lord your God, am a jealous God, punishing the children for the sin of the parents to the third and fourth generation of those who hate me." If these scriptures about generational curses are accurate, it's likely many of us carry such burdens without even realizing it. The wonderful truth is that we can break these curses. God's Word offers forgiveness for all sins: "If we confess our sins, He is faithful and just and will forgive us our sins and purify us from all unrighteousness" (1 John 1:9).

It's also essential to extend forgiveness to others. Colossians 3:13 states, "Bear with each other and forgive one another if any of you has a grievance against someone. Forgive as the Lord forgave you." Holding onto unforgiveness can obstruct our blessings, and this principle is intertwined with the process of releasing generational curses. Mark 11:25-26 reminds us that if we are praying and harboring grievances against others, we must forgive them first to ensure our prayers are not hindered.

Returning to the topic of generational curses, once we've sought forgiveness, I find great comfort in Exodus 20:6, which states, "but showing love to a thousand generations of those who love me and keep my commandments." This is a powerful reminder that we can break the chains of generational curses and instead pass down blessings for generations to come.

Recently, I've noticed many people discussing the injustices faced by their ancestors. It's fascinating to hear them say things like, "Your people did this or that" or "Christians have done this or that." You can fill in the blank whether people are talking about particular people, race, culture, religion, government, or even politics. I listen without judgment, understanding that they might not be in a place to hear my perspective. My family immigrated to America with my great-grandparents, so when someone says, "you people," it doesn't refer to me or my lineage. Yet, God has shown me how individuals can become trapped in generational curses by clinging to past traumas, wanting to share their pain with anyone willing to listen.

My heart aches for the suffering in the world, which is why I chose to become a counselor and coach—a calling I cherish deeply. However, holding onto unforgiveness and dragging past traumas into the present only perpetuates these burdens for future generations. We must find the courage to release and forgive the traumas of the past to pave the way for a new future—one filled with love and peace, both for ourselves and for others. This is how we can effect real change for generations to come.

There's an adage that says if we don't remember history, we are doomed to repeat it. However, what it really means is that if we fail to learn from the lessons of history, we will continue to repeat the same mistakes. In every moment, we have a choice: Do we dwell in the past, or do we create the life and world we envision for our children and grandchildren? I want to be part of a movement that chooses to create a new legacy.

To aid in breaking generational curses, I often share a prayer that I feel God gave me from a combination of sources, and I also use for myself and teach others:

"Father God, I ask for your forgiveness and for the clearing of any curses I have spoken or enacted against myself, any curses I have spoken or enacted against others and any curses spoken or enacted against me or my family across all generations—everywhere back on my mother's side, everywhere back on my father's side and every generation forward, across all DNA, across all genetics, across all time, space and reality, in Jesus' name." I recommend repeating this prayer three times.

When working with individuals or even for my own personal healing, I might focus on specific areas such as clutter, anger, heart issues, or other issues the person or the family has struggled with. In such cases, I would say something like: "Father, I ask for your forgiveness and for the clearing of any curses related to procrastination, addiction, anger, or clutter—everything I have spoken or done against myself, anything I have spoken or done against anyone else, and anything that has been spoken or done against me in this area, across all family lines, all generations—everywhere back on my mother's side, everywhere back on my father's side, and every generation forward, across all DNA, across all genetics, across all time, space and reality, in Jesus' name."

This process of prayer and intention can be a powerful step toward breaking free from the past and creating a brighter future for us and those who come after us.

Practice: List out curses you want to release from your life, and then practice the above with each, and notice how you feel.

Clutter

Another significant obstacle to receiving blessings is clutter. It's been said that clutter occupies mental space and generates negative energy both in the environment and in the minds of those around it. Research has shown that clutter can adversely affect mental health in various ways. For instance, it often increases stress levels, as disorganized surroundings can create a sense of chaos. This heightened stress is linked to elevated cortisol levels, which can have detrimental effects on overall well-being.

Moreover, clutter can hinder focus and productivity. Excessive visual distractions overwhelm the brain, making it difficult to concentrate on tasks at hand. It can also lead to decision fatigue; when faced with too many choices, individuals may find themselves paralyzed by indecision or resorting to procrastination. Additionally, clutter can disrupt memory by inhibiting the brain's ability to process and store information effectively. Living in cluttered spaces often breeds negative emotions such as guilt and frustration, further impacting mental health. I know, for me, if there is clutter, I will often feel the weight of something that needs to be done or fixed. Which takes up room in my brain and weighs on my energy. In contrast, a tidy environment fosters a sense of calm and enhances cognitive function and mood, highlighting the benefits of maintaining an organized space.

The Word of God also addresses the consequences of neglecting our surroundings and how it can rob us of the blessings in our lives. In Proverbs 24:30-34, we read: "I went past the field of a sluggard, past the vineyard of someone who has no sense; thorns had come up everywhere, the ground was covered with weeds, and the stone wall was in ruins. I applied my heart to what I observed and learned a lesson from what I saw: a little sleep, a little slumber, a little folding of the hands to rest—and poverty will come on you like a thief and scarcity like an armed man."

I appreciate the analogy that you cannot receive with full hands. If your hands are cluttered with items or even negative thoughts or emotions that no longer serve you, it's wise to dispose of them. If it's items, you could give them to someone in need or donate them. This act of letting go creates space for you to be open to the blessings that God has in store for you. By clearing out the old, you make room for the new, allowing for a more fulfilling, aligned, and purposeful life.

Exercise: After reading this section, what clutter do you need to clean up or remove? List each one and then do the action steps to release them. Then, notice how you feel. Write what this was like for you.

_____

_____

_____

_____

_____

_____

_____

_____

_____

_____

Sin Disrupts the Flow of Blessing

Sin is often misunderstood. It's not just about doing "bad things"—it's anything that causes us to operate outside of alignment with God's heart, His Word, and His Spirit. Sin distorts clarity. It creates static in the connection between our purpose and our peace.

When we hold on to unforgiveness, jealousy, pride, bitterness, rebellion, or fear, we create invisible walls that block the flow of God's blessings. Just as trauma alters the wiring of the brain, unconfessed sin and spiritual disconnection dull our sensitivity to God's voice. Our brains operate in confusion rather than peace, defensiveness rather than trust, and chaos rather than clarity.

God wants more for you. His call to repentance is not condemnation—it's an invitation. When we get honest, confess, and come into alignment, our brains and spirits find rest.

"Jesus replied, 'Very truly I tell you, no one can see the kingdom of God unless they are born again.'" — John 3:3 (NIV)

Being born again means stepping into a brand-new identity. It's more than behavior change—it's heart transformation. And when we allow God to clean the clutter in our lives, His blessings begin to flow freely. This isn't about condemnation, it's about alignment.

"If we confess our sins, He is faithful and just and will forgive us our sins and purify us from all unrighteousness." — 1 John 1:9 (NIV)

"But your iniquities have separated you from your God; your sins have hidden his face from you, so that he will not hear." — Isaiah 59:2 (NIV)

Sin separates. Repentance restores. The brain also responds. As we align with truth and walk in forgiveness and humility, the brain begins to heal from shame and fear. Dopamine and serotonin levels rise. Stress decreases. Peace returns.

I don't sit here in judgment, for I, too, have had many confessions of sin in my life. Even sins of being mean to myself and critical of my body. Emotional eating, denying myself food, not as a fast but as a punishment for what I didn't like. I have said things that I had to apologize for lots over the years. I have repented for prideful thoughts. I have put things as my idol, like my phone, TV, or even work which can continue to pop up at times. I have put others before God. I have not listened to God and been rebellious. None of us are without sin. Many times, the sins we hold are more against how we've treated ourselves or even mad at ourself that it's still a problem, far more than against others. I feel like most people recognize when they have sinned against others more easily than against themselves. This is not about pointing fingers to make us feel shame, but helping us clear things that create a hindrance to the blessings God has in store for us. It's about a remembrance that sin is, of course, contrary to our abundant blessings and peace.

Action Steps to Clear What Needs to Be Cleared

1. **Ask God to reveal hidden sin**: Pray Psalm 139:23-24: "Search me, God, and know my heart..."

_____

_____

_____

_____

2. **Write a spiritual inventory**: List what's out of alignment—thoughts, behaviors, relationships.

_____

_____

_____

_____

3. **Confess and surrender**: Speak it aloud in prayer. Repentance isn't about shame—it's about freedom.

_____

_____

_____

_____

4. **Receive grace**: Don't pick the guilt back up. You are washed clean. List out affirming scriptures that reflect that you are forgiven.

_____

_____

_____

_____

5. **Replace lies with truth**: What lie did the sin whisper? What does God say instead?

_____

_____

_____

_____

6. **Align with obedience**: Take one action step that aligns you back to God's heart.

_____

_____

_____

_____

7. **Speak your new identity daily**: "I am born again. I walk in truth. I receive the fullness of God's blessing." Rewrite these affirmations or others that align with your new identity.

_____

_____

_____

_____

When your heart is clear, your mind becomes clear. When your spirit is aligned, blessings flow freely. God is ready to restore what sin tried to steal. All He asks is your yes.

Conclusion

As we explore the journey toward manifesting a blessed life, it's essential to examine our own lives for any potential obstacles that may be hindering our blessings. By identifying and removing these barriers, we open ourselves up to a greater flow of abundance. Remember, God desires for you to experience a life filled with blessings. As you work to eliminate these hindrances, you will find blessings arriving in ways you never thought possible. His love for you is profound, and He truly wants the best for your life. Embrace this process and watch as your life transforms in miraculous ways.

"You can't change patterns by doing nothing to make new ones. Your brain either fires what you wire or the brain fires patterns from your past." —Erica Elliott

Reflection Notes

CHAPTER 10

Developing a Manifestation Routine

Bringing your goals and dreams to fruition necessitates more than occasional attempts; it demands a dedicated and intentional practice that weaves together both biblical teachings and scientific insights. Establishing a manifestation routine not only sharpens your focus but also aligns your daily actions with your most profound desires and beliefs. In this chapter, we will delve into how to craft a daily routine that embraces these guiding principles. You'll find examples of effective manifestation practices, along with tips for maintaining consistency and motivation. Additionally, we will include interactive questions designed to help you tailor your journey to your unique aspirations. It's great to release our past, but it's equally important to create new patterns in its place.

Daily Routines Incorporating Biblical and Scientific Principles

Creating a manifestation routine involves integrating the wisdom of the Bible, guidance from God, and your spirit with scientific practices that enhance mental and emotional well-being. Here's how you can combine these elements into your daily routine.

1. Morning Gratitude and Prayer

Start your day with gratitude and prayer. Begin by thanking God for the blessings in your life and asking for guidance and strength for the day ahead. This can set a positive tone in aligning your thoughts with a higher purpose.

- **Question:** What are five things you are grateful for today?
- **Scripture:** Choose a scripture to focus on. Example: "Give thanks in all circumstances; for this is God's Will for you in Christ Jesus" (1 Thessalonians 5:18).

- **Practice:** Spend 3 to 5 minutes in prayer, expressing gratitude and setting your intentions for the day.

2. Affirmations and Visualization

Use positive affirmations and visualizations to reinforce your goals and desires. Affirmations are positive statements that reflect your aspirations, while visualization involves creating a mental image of achieving your goals.

- **Question:** What is one affirmation that reflects your current goal?
- **Scripture:** What's a scripture that resonates with this? "He gives strength to the weary and increases the power of the weak" (Isaiah 40:29).
- **Practice:** Write down your affirmation and repeat it aloud several times. Spend a few minutes visualizing yourself achieving your goal and engaging all of your senses to make it vivid.

3. Meditation and Scripture Reading

Dedicate time to read and meditate on God's Word. Choose scriptures that resonate with your goals and reflect on their meanings and application in your life.

- **Question:** What is a scripture that speaks to you about your current journey?
- **Scripture:** "Your word is a lamp for my feet, a light for my path" (Psalms 119:105).
- **Practice:** Read a passage of scripture and spend a few minutes meditating on it. Ask God to reveal insights and guidance.

4. Mindfulness and Reflection

Incorporate mindfulness practices to stay present in a way throughout the day. Reflect on your thoughts and emotions, ensuring they align with your goals and faith.

- **Question:** How can you bring more mindfulness into your daily activities?

- **Scripture:** "Be still and know that I am God" (Psalm 46:10).
- **Practice:** Take short mindfulness breaks during the day to check in with your thoughts and emotions. Practice deep breathing and focus on the present moment. If you were feeling a certain undesirable emotion, one of my favorite tools is to say to yourself "I allow myself to feel this feeling, even though I don't want to feel this feeling." Allowing yourself to feel emotions without judging them is a great way to release them.

5. Evening Review and Gratitude

End your day by reviewing your progress and expressing your gratitude, reflecting on what went well and areas for improvement. Thank God for his guidance and blessings.

- **Question:** What was a highlight of your day, and what are you grateful for? I encourage using a method I call the "3 x 3 Appreciation Connection" that helps me, and I implement it with my clients: List three things that you are grateful for or good things that happened to you, and three things that you personally did well.
- **Scripture:** "And we know that in all things, God works for the good of those who love him, who have been called according to his purpose" (Romans 8:28).
- **Practice:** Spend a few minutes journaling about your day, noting any accomplishments or positive experiences. End with a prayer of gratitude.

Examples of Effective Manifestation Routines

To help you get started, here are a few examples of manifestation routines that integrate both biblical and scientific principles:

Example 1: The 20-Minute Morning Routine

- Gratitude and Prayer (5 minutes): Begin a prayer of gratitude, thanking God for a new day and blessings in your life.

- Affirmations and Visualization (5 Minutes): Write down three affirmations and repeat them aloud. Spend a few minutes visualizing your goals as if they have already been achieved. Make sure to add all five senses in your visualization.
- Scripture Reading and Meditation (5 minutes): Read a passage from the Bible and meditate on its meaning and application in your life.
- Mindfulness Practice (5 minutes): Conclude with a short mindfulness exercise, such as deep breathing or a body scan, to ground yourself for the day ahead.

Example 2: The Mid-Day Boost

- Gratitude Journal (3 minutes): Write or think about three things you are grateful for during your lunch break.
- Scripture Reflection (3 minutes): Read a short scripture and reflect on how it applies to your current situation.
- Affirmation Reminder (3 minutes): Repeat your affirmations and visualize your goals for a few minutes to recharge your motivation.

Example 3: The Evening Wind-Down

- Evening Review (10 Minutes): Reflect on your day, noting any successes in areas for growth and blessings you received, and write down your own thoughts in the journal as well.
- Prayer and Gratitude (5 minutes): End the day with a prayer, thanking God for his guidance and asking for a restful sleep.
- Scripture Meditation (5 minutes): Read and meditate on a calming scripture, allowing its peace to fill your mind and heart.

Tips for Staying Consistent and Motivated

Consistency and motivation play vital roles in sustaining a manifestation routine. Many individuals find themselves trapped in the belief that they must achieve perfection. I've experienced this myself. What I strive to teach—and what I aim to remind myself—is that the pursuit of perfection often stems from a trauma response. When we've been conditioned to believe that we must adhere to certain standards or risk rejection, those thoughts can replay in our minds like a deeply ingrained program, convincing us that we need to be flawless for our efforts to be deemed valid or worthwhile. Even as you reflect on the above examples, allow yourself to think about what feels better for you. Try one of the routines and tune in if it fits for you, and if it doesn't, how could you make one fit better for you? There isn't a set way that is the only way. Ask God to give you wisdom for what would work better for you.

As you embark on the journey of forming new habits, it's crucial to practice self-compassion. Remember to be gentle with yourself throughout this process. I often remind myself of the mantra, "Practice makes permanence," and I encourage my clients to adopt this mindset as well. Embrace the journey, allowing room for growth and learning, and you'll find that progress will come in time.

Here are some tips to help you stay on track:

1. **Set Clear Intentions:** When establishing your routine, it's essential to be specific about your goals. Clear intentions serve as your guiding light, providing both direction and purpose. I often liken this process to setting a GPS for your journey: when you input your desired destination, you can easily determine whether you're on the right path or veering off course. Without a clear sense of where you want to go, you may find yourself drifting aimlessly through life, experiencing moments of joy and despair without fully grasping the reasons behind them. Defining your objectives helps you navigate your journey with clarity and confidence.

   Question: What is your main goal for incorporating a manifestation routine? What are the outcomes you want to see and feel?

   _____

   _____

   _____

_____

_____

_____

_____

_____

_____

_____

2. **Create a Schedule:** Establish a regular schedule for your routine and stick to it. I always encourage people to put this on their calendar. When you put something on your calendar just like with your work, you will do something because it's important. Consistency is crucial for building habits.

   Question: What time of day works best for your routine?

_____

_____

_____

_____

_____

_____

_____

_____

_____

3. **Start Small:** Begin with manageable steps and gradually build up. Just like working out, you don't start with 100lb weights; you start small with 3lb or maybe 1lb weights. I have truly learned a lot about using micro steps in my life to create lasting change. After getting really sick with a health crash, all I could do was take micro steps. (I review more about my micro-step journey in the book *Her Healthy Glow: Embrace Wellness and Radiate Confidence From Inside Out* on Amazon, along with other great tips from many amazing authors.) Overcommitting can lead to burnout. You may want to start out committing to 15 minutes a day at first, then working your way up.

Question: Put it on your calendar now where you can spend 10–15 minutes doing these new routines. Reflect on what worked and what needs a bit of a change.

_____

_____

_____

_____

_____

_____

_____

_____

_____

4. **Track Your Progress:** Keep a journal to document your journey. Tracking progress can boost motivation and highlight areas of improvement. Tracking our progress can also lead to positive chemicals

like dopamine being released in our brains when we do the right things. Which, in turn, creates us wanting to do more of those things. It also shifts our focus to what we're doing right and gives us a better feeling of control in our lives.

Question: How will you track your progress?

_____

_____

_____

_____

_____

_____

_____

_____

5. **Stay Flexible:** Life can be unpredictable, so be flexible with your routine. Adjust as needed without feeling guilty.

Question: How can you adapt your routine when unexpected events occur?

_____

_____

_____

_____

_____

_____

_____

_____

_____

_____

6. **Seek Accountability:** Share your goals with a friend, get a coach, or join a group for support and accountability.

   Question: Whom can you share your journey with for support?

_____

_____

_____

_____

_____

_____

_____

_____

7. **Stay Inspired:** Surround yourself with inspiration, whether through books, podcasts, coaching groups, or people who uplift you.

   Question: What do you need, and who inspires you to keep going?

_____

_____

_____

_____

_____

_____

_____

_____

_____

8. **Reward Yourself:** Take the time to celebrate your successes, no matter how minor they may seem. Recognizing your achievements reinforces positive behavior and encourages continued progress. I cherish the phrase, "Be your own cheerleader," as it serves as a reminder to uplift yourself, especially when others may not be there to acknowledge your victories. This practice not only boosts our self-esteem but also reinforces the understanding that we possess the inner strength and capability to create a vibrant, positive, and blessed life. Embracing self-encouragement allows us to appreciate our journey and the growth that comes with it. I will say be cautious not to use food or drinks as a reward, which could lead to some unhealthy habits.

Question: How will you reward yourself for sticking to your routine?

_____

_____

_____

_____

_____

_____

_____

_____

_____

_____

Interactive Questions to Personalize Your Journey

To make this journey truly your own, reflect on the following questions and jot down your answers:

1. What are three goals you want to manifest?

_____

_____

_____

_____

_____

2. Which scriptures resonate most with your goal?

_____

_____

_____

_____

_____

_____

3. How can you incorporate gratitude into your daily routine?

_____

_____

_____

_____

_____

4. What positive affirmations will you use to reinforce your goals?

_____

_____

_____

_____

_____

5. What time of day will you dedicate to scripture reading and meditation?

_____

_____

_____

_____

_____

_____

6. How can you incorporate mindfulness into your daily activities?

_____

_____

_____

_____

_____

_____

7. What will you include in your evening review and gratitude practice?

_____

_____

_____

_____

_____

8. What tools, people, or supplies do you need to be successful?

_____

_____

_____

Conclusion

Creating a manifestation routine that blends both biblical teachings and scientific principles offers a powerful means to align your thoughts, actions, and faith with your aspirations. By establishing a consistent practice, you lay a solid groundwork for bringing your desires to fruition and realizing your dreams. It's important to remain adaptable, monitor your progress, and seek support when necessary. As you embark on this transformative journey, remember that consistency and dedication are essential for turning your aspirations into reality. Embrace the process, trust in God's plan, and witness the beauty that unfolds as your life aligns with your highest goals and divine purpose.

Reflection Notes

CHAPTER 11

Living a Manifested, Blessed Life

Embracing a manifested, blessed life involves embodying the principles and practices that help you align with your goals and dreams. It's about maintaining success while continuously growing, transforming, and harmonizing your life with God's Will, your potential, and the insights of science. In this chapter, we will delve into long-term strategies for sustaining manifestation and success, sharing personal stories and testimonies of lives that have been transformed. Additionally, we'll offer encouragement and valuable insights on living in accordance with God's laws and the principles of brain science. As you dive into shifting and changing your thoughts and actions, I often like to say: do all of this as if you were a little child getting curious and playful in life, trusting God to lead and guide you to the most amazingly blessed, abundant life.

Scriptures on Childlike Faith, Humility, and Spiritual Alignment

1. Matthew 19:14 (NIV)

"Jesus said, 'Let the little children come to me, and do not hinder them, for the kingdom of heaven belongs to such as these.'"

Why it matters: Jesus doesn't just permit children to come—He declares that the Kingdom belongs to those like them: humble, trusting, open-hearted.

2. Mark 10:15 (NIV)

"Truly I tell you, anyone who will not receive the kingdom of God like a little child will never enter it."

Why it matters: Receiving the Kingdom like a child isn't about immaturity—it's about spiritual purity, dependence, and surrender.

3. Luke 18:17 (NIV)

"Truly I tell you, anyone who will not receive the kingdom of God like a little child will never enter it."

Why it matters: This repeats the same truth across the gospels. God emphasizes simplicity and trust over striving and pride. I think about my little granddaughter and grandson who are almost three and they say often, that's mine or my mommy, my toy, my papa, my gaga. They make declarations too.

4. John 3:5 (NIV)

"Jesus answered, 'Very truly I tell you, no one can enter the kingdom of God unless they are born of water and the Spirit.'"

Why it matters: Being born again is a spiritual rebirth—starting over with a childlike, Spirit-led heart. Water from the Spirit well - NEVER runs dry.

5. 1 Peter 2:2 (NIV)

"Like newborn babies, crave pure spiritual milk, so that by it you may grow up in your salvation."

Why it matters: This speaks to the ongoing need for spiritual nourishment and a teachable heart—hallmarks of childlike posture before God. This is why it is so important to go to the Bible and plant the seeds of God's Word in our lives.

6. Hebrews 5:12-14 (NIV)

"12 In fact, though by this time you ought to be teachers, you need someone to teach you the elementary truths of God's word all over again. You need milk, not solid food!

13 Anyone who lives on milk, being still an infant, is not acquainted with the teaching about righteousness.

14 But solid food is for the mature, who by constant use have trained themselves to distinguish good from evil."

Why it matters: This passage emphasizes the importance of spiritual maturity and moving beyond basic teachings to deeper understanding. The Bible is a teaching of Remembering - Who You Are, Who's You Are, and All of the Power you have through the Spirit - Wielding the Sword "God's Word" as the Warrior you are called to be. That's why God called me to write this book to remind you of His Word - His Promises - His Love!

Join me on this journey toward a life filled with purpose and fulfillment.

Regular Reflection and Adjustments

Ongoing reflection and adjustment are essential to ensure that your manifestation practices stay effective and aligned with your evolving goals. Keep in mind that this is your journey, and you have the power to make changes as you see fit. It's not about relinquishing control; rather, it's about setting your internal GPS and taking the proactive steps that guide you toward a richly blessed and manifested life. Embrace the journey with intention and watch as you navigate toward your dreams with clarity and purpose. By now, you have probably noticed I ask you to write down your goals, reflect on God's Word and prayer, and practice, then check and realign over and over as needed. All of the steps I have guided you through are brain science tools to help reinforce more of what you want in the brain. I often have individuals get stuck on the action part once they figure out the goal.

One thing that God has really taught me is that sometimes, we need to take a step of faith, moving towards the goal before he gives us more information. That's exactly what happened to me as a writer. This is actually the first book that I wrote for publishing; however, since republishing this month, I will have published seven other books, and by the end of this year, around a dozen. I was terrified, as I talked about at the beginning of this book, about writing this book, not just because of how people look at manifestation, but also putting myself out there as a writer. Besides dealing with having a brain injury, I struggled with imposter syndrome in this particular area of my life. Imposter syndrome is a cognitive dissonance experience that occurs in individuals who are highly successful in one or more areas but feel almost paralyzed or inadequate in others. I don't believe that was just because of my brain injury either. This was something I had struggled with before, and I write about this more in a book called *Her Path to Entrepreneurship*. In that book, I share a little more about imposter syndrome, and also the steps that I took to clear the mess in my own mind and take the leap of faith as a writer. I have worked with many individuals helping them with imposter syndrome, but I also had to work on this area myself.

After I cleared the block that came from my past, I was able to take steps forward, and as they say, the rest is history. A lot of people say, "What if I get it wrong?" To this, I would say when you take a risk of pain, it's similar to what happened for us in the military when we would qualify our weapons. You would take the rifle, look down at the target, and fire at it. Then, if you were off, you would adjust your scope and re-fire. Just like in life, if you miss the target, then you recalibrate your scope by tuning back inside of you and asking God to give you guidance and the steps to move forward. Then you take the steps, and little by little, you get better and better with your guidance system and knowing with the above tools when you are on track or off track and just need a little tweak to get back on track.

Exercise: Set aside time each week to reflect on your progress. Ask yourself the following questions:

1. What are my goals?

_____

_____

_____

_____

_____

_____

2. What action steps did I take this week?

_____

_____

_____

_____

_____

_____

3. What successes have I achieved this week?

_____

_____

_____

_____

_____

_____

4. What prayers have been answered?

_____

_____

_____

_____

_____

_____

5. What challenges did I face, and how did I overcome them?

_____

_____

_____

_____

_____

_____

6. What adjustments can I make to improve my manifestations?

_____

_____

_____

_____

_____

7. What do I want... (clearly stated)?

_____

_____

_____

_____

_____

_____

8. What are some steps I can take this week to get there?

_____

_____

_____

_____

_____

_____

Lifelong Learning

Embrace a commitment to lifelong learning and personal development. Cultivate a sense of curiosity and remain open to new insights that foster your growth and adaptability. You are not the same person you were ten, twenty, or even thirty years ago; every stage of life brings new experiences and lessons. By recognizing that you are constantly evolving and learning, you empower yourself to take charge of your own growth, leading to more favorable outcomes. You'll come to realize that you are indeed the architect of your life, and you possess the strength to shape your reality. You will, however, need to tune in often to make sure you are on track and in alignment with your clear goals and purpose. In my practice working with individuals, I often will say, "Maybe you're just 5 degrees off." I learned a valuable lesson when I was learning to fly a plane. When flying an airplane, if you have your compass directionally set 5 degrees off and you were flying, say, to California, you may find yourself in Canada, which is a pretty big deal. Checking and re-checking yourself is not a bad thing. The more you learn to turn in words, tune into God and into your spirit, asking yourself if you feel like you're on track or off, keeps you headed in the right direction to manifesting a blessed life that God intends for you.

Question: What new skills or knowledge can you pursue to enhance your manifestation journey?

_____

_____

_____

_____

_____

_____

Exercise: Identify a book, course, or workshop that aligns with your goals and commit to engaging with it regularly.

_____

_____

_____

_____

_____

Consistent Practice of Gratitude and Positivity

Gratitude and positivity are powerful tools for maintaining a high vibrational state, which is essential for manifestation. The Word of God teaches us to come into His presence with thanksgiving and praise.

Exercise: Keep a gratitude journal and write down five things you're grateful for every day. Reflect on how these blessings have contributed to your overall well-being and success.

_____

_____

_____

_____

_____

_____

Strengthen Your Faith

Deepen your faith through regular prayer, scripture reading, and meditation while trusting in God's plan and that He is here to help on your journey and provide a solid foundation for your manifestation practices.

Question: How can you strengthen your faith and deepen your connection with God? What areas of faith do you need to strengthen?

_____

_____

_____

_____

_____

_____

Get Connected with a Supportive Community

Surround yourself with individuals who share your vision and encourage you on your manifestation path. A solid network of support can provide the motivation and accountability you need for your personal growth. As mentioned earlier in this book, it is said that you tend to reflect the three to five people you spend the most time with. This is why it is crucial to select those who are also evolving, seeking knowledge, and engaging in similar practices. This mutual encouragement can enrich your journey together. The teachings of the Word of God remind us that when two individuals come together, if one stumbles, the other is there to help lift them up, fostering a powerful connection of support and strength. Plus, the Word of God reminds us that where two or more are gathered, there is power (Matthew 18:20).

Question: Who in your life supports your manifestation journey, and how can you connect with them more regularly? If you don't have someone, joining a group is a great way to have support and make friendships. I have a few groups on Facebook that you are welcome to join. (Manifesting God's Way, Virtual Bliss Meditation Group, and Energetic Elevation)

_____

_____

_____

_____

_____

_____

Embracing Challenges and Growth Opportunities

Embrace challenges as precious opportunities for personal growth and discovery. Overcoming these hurdles not only strengthens your resolve but also sharpens your ability to manifest your desires. Have you ever acquired a skill through one method, only to later uncover an alternative that yielded even better results? This has happened to me a lot in life. One area is technology and using certain apps. I can't even tell you how many times my daughter has shown me quicker, easier ways to do something on technology. This highlights the importance of continually learning and evolving our approach to life.

Consider life as an intricate journey, marked by clear objectives, where we can evaluate our progress much like a GPS guiding us on a road trip. Occasionally, we encounter roadblocks that prompt us to take a different route for better outcomes. Just as a GPS communicates real-time updates via satellite, tuning into our intuition with God can provide invaluable insights. When we veer off course, it's crucial to view this as a simple adjustment rather than a reason for judgment or condemnation. I truly believe this is why reading the Bible and allowing God to speak to us is so powerful. How many times have you read a verse and something new is revealed or in a different light or circumstance? Adopting this mindset enables us to steer back on track with greater ease and confidence. Give it a try!

Let me reiterate: it is persistence, not perfection, that creates permanence. If you find yourself off track, remember that this is not the time to be hard on yourself. Everyone strays sometimes—even those who seem to have it all together. The Word of God reminds us in Romans 7:19-27: "For I do not do the good I want to do, but the evil I do not want to do—this I keep on doing. Now, if I do what I do not want to do, it is no longer I who does it, but it is sin living in me that does it. So, I find this law at work: although I want to do good, evil is right there with me. In my inner being, I delight in God's law, but I see another law at work in me, waging war against the law of my mind and making me a prisoner of the law of sin at work within me. What a wretched man I am! Who will rescue me from this body that is subject to death? Thanks be to God, who delivers me through Jesus Christ, our Lord! So then, I myself in my mind am a slave to God's law, but in my sinful nature, a slave to the law of sin. Therefore, there is no condemnation for those who are in Christ Jesus, because through Christ Jesus, the law of the Spirit who gives life has set you free from the law of sin and death."

What does this mean? Read it closely. Paul addresses the struggle between the mind, body, and spirit, acknowledging that we will make mistakes. This internal conflict can be understood through the lens of neurobiology. The prefrontal cortex, which governs reasoning and decision-making, often finds itself at odds with the more primal responses generated by the amygdala. When faced with temptation or pressure, the amygdala can trigger emotional responses that lead us away from our intentions, creating a battle within us.

This is why we must continually return to God. Through His Word and the Holy Spirit, we are liberated from the law of sin and death. The rest is merely bondage of the mind and body. Neuroplasticity allows us to rewire these pathways, reinforcing healthier responses through persistent practice and reliance on God's guidance.

Which law do you choose to follow: God's law through the Spirit, which brings freedom, or man's law, which leads to sin and condemnation? It's essential to clarify that when the Bible mentions sin, it refers to actions that are not in alignment with God's laws—actions that hinder our ability to live a healthy, blessed, and abundant life. When we engage in behaviors that diverge from these laws, the brain's reward system, particularly the release of dopamine, can mislead us into temporary satisfaction, reinforcing patterns that ultimately lead to regret and discontent. This is why understanding the consequences of our choices is crucial.

Often, religious discussions around sin can feel judgmental, painting it as the worst thing one can do. However, consider that sin simply indicates a divergence from God's laws or even separation from God or a separation for our highest good that leads to blessings and abundance. Viewing sin in this light allows for a more compassionate understanding of our struggles. The anterior cingulate cortex, responsible for error detection and emotional regulation, plays a key role here. It helps us recognize when we are out of alignment and encourages us to return to the path of righteousness.

Allow yourself to see sin as a term that signifies being out of alignment with God's laws rather than a source of condemnation. Recognize that the path to an abundant and blessed life on earth involves aligning ourselves with God's laws through His Word and the Spirit. This alignment can create a taste of heaven on earth. As we practice this alignment, we can strengthen the neural pathways associated with positive behaviors and choices, allowing us to cultivate a more fulfilling life rooted in faith and love.

Our minds can develop patterns that do not serve us well. To shift and change these patterns, we must gain clarity about the paths that hinder our greatest good.

Question: What recent challenge have you faced? Where are you off track? What did you learn from it? What will you choose to do differently?

_____

_____

_____

_____

_____

_____

Exercise: Reflect on a time someone taught you how to do something with more ease or success, and write it down. What did you learn from it? Reflect on current challenges and identify steps you can take to overcome them. Write down the lessons you learn and how they can contribute to your growth.

_____

_____

_____

_____

_____

_____

Personal Stories and Case Studies of Transformed Lives

Hearing about other successes can be incredibly inspiring and motivating. Here are some personal stories and testimonies of individuals who have transformed their lives through manifestation practices.

Sarah's Journey to Financial Freedom

Sarah was struggling with debt and financial insecurity. She decided to apply manifestation principles to her financial situation. She started by visualizing herself living a debt-free life and used positive affirmations such as, "I am financially free and prosperous." She searched God's Word about money. She began memorizing and meditating on the scripture, "And God is able to bless you abundantly, so that in all things at all times, having all that you need, you will abound in every good work" (2 Corinthians 9:8).

Sarah also began a gratitude practice, thanking God for the financial blessings she already had. She began noticing more blessings that represented money blessings in her life, like coupons, discounts, and unexpected gifts. She created a vision board with images representing financial abundance and reviewed it daily. Over time, Sarah's mindset shifted from scarcity to abundance. She found a new job opportunity, managed her expenses better, and gradually paid off her debt.

John's Transformation Health and Wellness

John struggled with poor health and low energy for years. He decided to take control of his health using manifestation techniques. John started visualizing himself as healthy, vibrant, and full of energy. He repeated affirmations like, "I am healthy, strong, and full of vitality. Every day in every way I'm getting better and stronger."

He searched God's Word and incorporated scripture into his routine, focusing on verses like Jeremiah 30:17, "But I will restore you to health and heal your wounds." He also began adopting healthier eating habits, exercising, and practicing mindfulness and meditation. He joined a group that supported his healthy lifestyle, where he could share and get support from others, and encourage others as well.

John's health improved significantly over time. He lost weight (body fat), gained muscle, and felt more energetic than ever. He made a commitment to living a manifested life through health and wellness practices.

Emily's Success in Career and Personal Fulfillment

Emily felt unfulfilled in her career and longed for a job that aligned with her passions. She decided to manifest her dream job by visualizing herself in a fulfilling role, repeating affirmations like, "I am doing work that I love and making a difference," and setting clear career goals. She went to God's Word to find out where God talks about purpose in life. She began to daily memorize and say the scripture, "For I know the plans I have for you, declares the Lord, plans to prosper you and not to harm you, plans to give you hope and a future" (Jeremiah 29:11).

Emily also prayed for guidance and wisdom, asking God to lead her to the right opportunities. She asked God to give her favor and open the right doors. She took proactive steps by networking, improving her skills, and applying for positions that matched her interests.

Eventually, Emily landed her dream job, where she felt valued and fulfilled. Her story is a testament to the power of combining faith, visualization, and proactive action to manifest career success.

Encouragement and Final Thoughts: Living According to God's Laws and Brain Science

Living a manifested life is an ongoing journey that requires faith, dedication, and a positive mindset. Here are some final thoughts and encouragement to help you stay on track:

1. Trust in God's Timing

Remember that God's timing is perfect. Sometimes, our desires manifest in ways we don't expect or at times we don't anticipate. Trust that God has a plan for you and that everything is working out for you.

Scripture: "Let us not become weary in doing good, for at the proper time we will reap a harvest if we do not give up" (Galatians 6:9).

Scripture: "When the time is right, I, the Lord, will make it happen" (Isaiah 60:22).

Scripture: "Do not be anxious about anything, but in every situation, by prayer and petition, with thanksgiving, present your request to God. And the peace of God, which transcends all understanding, will guard your hearts and your minds in Christ Jesus" (Philippians 4:6-7).

Scripture: "Rejoicing in Hope; patient and tribulation; continuing instant in prayer" (Romans 12:12).

Scripture: "But his delight is in the law of the Lord; and in his law day and night, he meditates day and night. And he shall be like a tree planted by the rivers of water, that brings its fruit in season; his leaf also shall not wither; and whatsoever he doeth it shall prosper" (Psalms 1:2-3).

2. Stay Positive and Persistent

Positivity and persistence are key to maintaining a manifestation mindset. Even when faced with challenges, keep your faith strong and stay committed to your goals. Write down a list of positive affirmations and scriptures and read them daily, especially when facing challenges. You can also go back over your gratitude journal and review the things that have already come to pass to remind you of the blessings that are working out for you.

Scripture: "Finally, brothers and sisters, whatever is true, whatever is noble, whatever is right, whatever is pure, whatever is lovely, whatever is admirable—if anything is excellent or praiseworthy—think about such things" (Philippians 4:8).

Scripture: "Do not conform to the pattern of this world but be transformed by the renewing of your mind. Then you'll be able to test and approve what God's Will is—his good, pleasing and perfect will" (Romans 12:2).

Scripture: "We demolish arguments in every petition that sets itself up against the knowledge of God, and we take captive every thought to make it obedient to Christ" (2 Corinthians 10:5).

Scripture: "The tongue has the power of life and death, and those who love it will eat its fruit" (Proverbs 18:21).

Scripture: "But they that wait upon the Lord shall renew their strength; shall mount up with wings as eagles; they shall run, and not be weary; they shall walk, and not faint" (Isaiah 40:31).

3. Embrace Continuous Growth

Personal growth and development are essential for sustaining manifestation success. Embrace new opportunities, learn from experiences, and keep evolving. Set a personal development goal, such as reading 15 minutes a day for learning and growing.

Scripture: "If any of you lacks wisdom, you should ask God, who gives generously to all without finding fault, and it will be given to you" (James 1:5).

Scripture: "Let the wise listen and add to their understanding, and let the discerning get guidance" (Proverbs 1:5).

Scripture: "Study to show their self-approved unto God, a Workman that needed it not to be ashamed, rightly dividing (handling) the word of truth" (2 Timothy 2:15).

Scripture: "Out of the same mouth come praise and cursing. My brothers and sisters, this should not be. Can both freshwater and saltwater flow from the same spring? My brothers and sisters, can a fig tree bear olives or a grapevine bear figs? Neither can a salt spring produce fresh water" (James 3:10-12).

4. Connect with Your Higher Purpose

Align your goals with your higher purpose and God's Will brings deeper fulfillment and meaning to your manifestation journey. Seek God's guidance and stay true to your values. Spend time in prayer and meditation, asking God to reveal your higher purpose and how you can align your actions with it.

Scripture: "For we are God's handiwork, created in Christ Jesus to do good work, which God prepared in advance for us to do" (Ephesians 2:10).

Scripture: "The thief comes only to steal and kill and destroy; I have come that they may have life and have it more abundantly" (John 10:10).

Scripture: "Commit to the Lord, whatever you do, and he will establish your plans" (Proverbs 16:3).

Scripture: "Where there is no vision, the people perish: but he that keep it, the law, happy is he" (Proverbs 29:18).

Scripture: "This book of the law shall not depart out of thigh mouth; but thou shall meditate there and day and night, that thou mass observed to do according to all that is written there in: for then thou shout make the way prosperous, and then thou shall have good success" (Joshua 1:8).

Every morning, my husband and I do a devotion and prayer. I thought I would share the prayer that we do. If it's something that you want to use, feel free. Parts of it have the Prayer of Jabez in it, and other parts are from God's Word as well.

"Father God, thank you for our lives. Thank you for our provisions and blessings. This is going to be a Great Day! I pray that you would bless us and our relationship and our kids and our grandkids and our family and our friends. Help us to be guided by our purpose. Help us to speak words of love and peace and joy, may we be mindful of the words that we speak for those words are sewing seeds, bless us, indeed, enlarge and expand our territories, help us to not cause harm to others, save us from our enemies, lead us not into temptation, but deliver us from evil, destroy the devour for our namesake and for your glory we pray that you would put a hedge of protection around all of us and put on us the armor of God (the helmet of salvation, the breast plate in the robe of righteousness, the shoes of peace, girth about our loins with truth, equip us with the sword of your Word). May we be guided in all that we say and do, may we be blessed with love, joy, peace, prosperity, health, and wealth, and may we be a blessing to others in Jesus' name, amen."

5. Celebrate Your Success

Celebrate your successes, no matter how small. Acknowledge your achievements and express gratitude for the progress you've made. Create a success journal where you document your achievements and reflect on the positive impact they've had on your life.

Scripture: "May we shout for joy over your victory and lift our banners in the name of our God" (Psalms 20:5).

Scripture: "But thanks be to God! He gives us victory through our Lord Jesus Christ" (1 Corinthians 15:57).

Scripture: "Go and enjoy choice food and sweet drinks, and send some to those who have nothing prepared. This day is sacred to our Lord. Do not grieve, for the joy of the Lord is your strength" (Nehemiah 8:10).

Scripture: "This is the day the Lord has made; let us rejoice and be glad in it" (Psalms 118:24).

Scripture: "Rejoice evermore. Pray without ceasing. And in everything give thanks: for this is the will of God in Christ Jesus concerning you" (1 Thessalonians 5:16-18).

Interactive Exercises

1. **Connect with God:** Take time every day, multiple times a day, beginning when you wake up, to pray and ask God, the Holy Spirit, and your guardian angels to guide you. Also, ask God to give you positive surprises throughout your day. Take note when this happens and give thanks to God. You will begin to notice the gifts He gives more often.

2. **Let Go:** Release things that no longer serve your highest good. Write out all the things that you want to let go of—things like unforgiveness, hurt, anger, fear, clutter, etc., and anything you are mad at yourself about, and anything you are upset with others about.

3. **Shifting a Negative State to a Positive State:** You might have come across the idea that it takes only 16 or 17 seconds to transition from a negative thought to a positive one in our brains. Upon discovering this, I began to consider how I could facilitate this shift for myself and my clients, making it more effective and lasting. When I encounter someone who is struggling—or even when I find myself in a similar situation—I often reach for a piece of paper to list 16 positive affirmations that counteract the negativity. I encourage my clients to do the same, and they tell me it works so incredibly well. This approach allows you to not just speak these affirmations, but also write them down, effectively reprogramming the brain for success.

    For example, if I find myself feeling frustrated with my husband, thinking he doesn't care about me, I take a moment to write down 16 reasons that demonstrate his love for me. Similarly, if I feel as though my life is chaotic and blessings seem hard to find, I'll compile a list of 16 positive occurrences that have come my way in the last week. By shifting my focus in this way and committing my thoughts to paper, I can transform my mindset and rewire my brain for a more positive outlook. This practice enables me to concentrate on my desires rather than my disappointments, empowering me to create a more rewarding and successful life experience.

4. **Rewire Your Brain:** For at least two weeks, pay attention to your words and eliminate the phrase "I don't want" and replace it with "I want." Your words are powerful. In James 3:10, we find, "Blessings and curses come from the tongue." The Word of God also tells us to take EVERY thought and make it obedient to Christ (2 Corinthians 10:5). Then, what is obedient to Christ? "Let all that you do be done in love" (1 Corinthians 16:14). That means to us and everyone else.

5. **Memorize Scripture:** Take one Bible scripture a week that you write out 3 times, meditate on it, and recite daily at least 10 times during the day.

6. **Affirmations:** Write out three affirmations that you place on your mirror, desk, refrigerator, or in your car that you repeat every time you see them. Each week, do three new affirmations.

7. **Write a Forgiveness Letter:** Select someone you wish to forgive. It can even be yourself. Take the time to write down all the pain they have caused you, expressing your feelings fully and honestly. Then, compose a letter as if you were addressing that person in their purest form, embodying the highest love and light they were meant to be before the weight of the world's programming altered them. In this letter, offer your understanding and compassion to them. Once you've completed both letters, release them by burning or shredding them, symbolizing your liberation from the past.

   Keep in mind that anything from the past is no longer present; these experiences are wounds we have the power to heal, even in the absence of the other person. It's about addressing what has become trapped within us and allowing ourselves to move forward toward healing and freedom. You may also find where you feel the unforgiven areas or the pain in your body or brain, and breathe in God's loving and light healing into that place in space until you've shifted or released it. Imagine handing it over to God, like piles of rocks, and allowing God to transform them.

8. **Support:** Find a coach, counselor, friend, mentor, or someone who you can have as an accountability person who holds the same higher beliefs and values that are a reflection of similar goals you have for your life. Connect with a supportive group—a Bible study group, friend group, coaching group, etc.—to practice living your manifested life. Remember, you become like the three to five people you spend the most time with.

9. **Use Smiling and Laughter Like Medicine:** Shift your mood—see a smile in your heart and a smile inside others' hearts, too. This is an amazing tool to link our brains to positive chemicals, shifting our

attitude and attention. It can be great to do for ourselves when we have pain in the body, too. Imagine seeing a smile in the part of your body that's hurting. Laugh for no reason at all to create a new chemical flow.

10. **Letter to Yourself:** Write a letter from your future self in six months, who has all of your goals and desires obtained. Example: "I'm grateful to now be enjoying ____." (You can do any future time writing, but six months is a good starting place because our ability to believe it is much easier than a week or a month until you practice more.)

11. **Record Yourself:** Record yourself reading your letter with enthusiasm, bring in all senses, exaggerate the experience, and listen to this every day until your desires come true. Then, listen to it daily when you first get up or when you go to bed, over and over again. Re-record a new one as needed.

12. **Foster an Abundance Mindset:** Look around your environment and notice and speak about abundance. Look at the threads of your clothes—you can't even count them all... There is ABUNDANCE. Look at the leaves on the trees—there is ABUNDANCE.

13. **Toolbox:** Put together a list of tools that help you go up the ladder of emotions that you can easily go to and use when you are having a tough day. Put this list in your phone, place a list on your desk, and have a list somewhere you can see it regularly. Update the list as needed.

Conclusion

Most importantly, take charge of creating the life you desire! Begin by immersing yourself in the feelings associated with the life you wish to lead. If your focus is solely on acquiring money or material possessions, achieving them may leave you feeling unfulfilled. This is why the Word of God encourages us to set our minds on higher things. Living a life of manifestation goes beyond merely reaching specific goals; it involves cultivating a mindset and lifestyle that resonates with your highest aspirations and divine purpose.

By blending biblical teachings with scientific methods into your everyday routine, you can achieve lasting success in manifestation and continue to grow and evolve. Trust in God's timing, maintain a positive outlook, and remain persistent. Embrace ongoing growth, connect with your higher purpose, and take time to celebrate your achievements. As you journey forward, remember that you are enveloped in God's love and wisdom, and you possess the power to shape a life that aligns with your most profound desires and values.

"Remember You Plot Your Future—Finding Peace and Love with Yourself and the Divine Creates the Healthy Place From which One can Grow and Glow." —Erica Elliot

Your Journey to Manifestation Recap

As we come to the end of this book, it's an opportunity to reflect on the journey we have shared. Together, we have delved into the powerful principles of manifestation, drawing from both biblical wisdom and scientific understanding. The insights and practices presented throughout these chapters aim to empower you to harmonize your thoughts, actions, and faith with your innermost desires and God's divine purpose.

Recap of the key points covered in the book:

1. **Foundations of Manifestation:** We started by understanding the definition and principles of manifestation and recognizing the power of intention, focus, belief, and action. Historical perspectives and biblical laws provided a robust framework for our journey.

2. **Biblical Principles of Manifestation:** We delved into key scriptures from the Bible that support manifestation, learning how these sacred texts can be applied to our daily lives to foster faith and positive change in manifesting our most blessed, abundant life.

3. **The Science of the Brain:** We uncovered how neuroscience supports positive thinking and visualization by exploring the brain's function

related to thoughts and beliefs, and understanding how the brain processes and stores information, which has equipped us with tools to enhance our manifestation practices.

4. **How the Brain Processes Information:** We explored how the brain stores, retrieves, and links information with emotions. This chapter highlighted the importance of renewing the mind through repetition and intentional tools, reinforcing how transformation happens through both faith and biology.

5. **Traumas, Tragedies, and Setbacks: Moving Through Pain into Purpose:** We examined how trauma impacts the brain and the spirit and offered biblical insight alongside practical tools for healing. This chapter provided empowering strategies rooted in faith to help turn pain into purpose and move forward with strength.

6. **Aligning Your Thoughts with God's Word:** Techniques for aligning our thoughts with biblical scriptures, the role of meditation in prayer, and inspirational case studies illustrated the transformative power of spiritual alignment.

7. **Practical Applications of Brain Science:** We examined methods for leveraging brain science in manifestation, including effective visualization techniques and creating and using vision boards.

8. **Overcoming Doubts and Negative Thoughts:** To confront and identify challenging, limiting beliefs, a powerful biblical strategy is to seek out scriptures that directly oppose those beliefs. Begin by researching relevant Bible verses and then articulate your new belief based on God's Word. For instance, you might affirm, "According to God's Word, I will be anxious for nothing, and I can do all things through Christ who empowers me." Writing down these scriptures serves as an effective tool to counteract doubt and negativity. This practice not only reinforces a positive mindset but also equips us with the psychological strategies needed to overcome mental barriers.

Embrace this approach to transform your thinking and strengthen your faith.

9. **Eliminating Blocks to Blessings:** Delving into the obstacles that may hinder your blessings—such as unforgiveness, physical clutter, the words we use, generational barriers—is an essential step toward personal growth. Recognizing these blocks and utilizing effective tools to release them is important. By addressing these issues head-on, you can clear the path for abundant blessings to flow into your life. Embrace this journey of exploration and healing, transforming challenges into opportunities for renewal and empowerment.

10. **Developing a Manifestation Routine:** We outlined daily routines that incorporate both biblical and scientific principles, offering examples of effective practices and tips for staying consistent and motivated with intentional practices.

11. **Living a Manifested Life:** Finally, we explored long-term strategies for sustaining manifestation and success, shared personal stories of transformation, and provided encouragement to live a life aligned with God's laws and brain science.

Encouragement to Start the Journey of Manifesting God's Way

Your journey to manifestation is a personal and transformative path that aligns your desires with divine purpose and scientific understanding. As you embark on this journey, remember that the key to success lies in consistency, faith, tuning into your spirit, asking God's help, and equipping a positive forward mindset. Trust in God's timing and wisdom, stay committed to your practices, and remain open to growth and learning. Remember, the only way you get good at something is by practicing it. Manifesting a blessed, abundant life is about practicing skills.

Embrace each day as an opportunity to manifest your dreams and goals. Celebrate your progress, no matter how small, and view challenges as opportunities for growth. Surround yourself with a supportive community and continually seek inspiration and guidance from God's Word.

You have the power to create a life that reflects your deepest aspirations and aligns with your highest purpose. With faith, determination, and the tools and techniques shared in this book, you are well equipped to manifest a life of abundance, joy, and fulfillment.

Reflection Notes

Additional Resources and Further Readings

To continue your journey and deepen your understanding, here are some additional resources and further reading:

Appendix A: Key Bible Scriptures for Manifestation

Mark 11:24 – "Therefore I tell you, whatever you ask for in prayer, believe that you have received it, and it will be yours."

Matthew 17:20 – "He replied, 'Because you have so little faith. Truly, I tell you, if you have faith as small as a mustard seed, you can say to this mountain, move from here to there, and it will move. Nothing will be impossible for you.'"

Proverbs 23:7 – "For as he thinks in his heart, so is he."

Philippians 4:13 – "I can do all things through Christ who strengthens me."

Romans 12:2 – "Do not conform to the pattern of this world, but be transformed by the renewing of your mind. Then you will be able to test and improve what God's Will is—his good, pleasing, and perfect will."

Hebrews 11:1 – "Now faith is confidence in what we hope for and assurance about what we do not see."

John 14:13-14 – "And I will do whatever you ask in my name, so that the Father may be glorified in the Son. You may ask me for anything in my name, and I will do it."

Appendix B: Recommended Books and Articles on Brain Science, Spirituality, and Manifestation

Books:

The Power of Positive Thinking by Norman Vincent Peale
Man's Search for Meaning by Viktor Frankl

Battlefield of the Mind by Joyce Meyer

As a Man Thinketh by James Allen

Rags to Riches by Tom Leding

E-Squared" by Pam Grout

Polyvagal Theory in Therapy by Deb Dana

The Body Keeps Score by Bessel Van Der Klock, M.D.

Mindsight by Dan Siegel, M.D.

Think and Grow Rich by Napoleon Hill

Switch on Your Brain by Dr. Caroline Leaf

Bible—*New International Version* and *King James Version*

The Biology of Belief by Bruce H Lipton, Ph.D.

You Are The Placebo by Dr. Joe Dispenza

The Brain Changes Itself by Norman Doidge, M.D.

How God Changes Your Brain by Andrew Newberg, M.D. and Mark Robert Waldman

When God Doesn't Make Sense by James Dobson, PHd.

Articles, Journals, and Other Resources:

"The Neuroscience of Gratitude and How it Affects Anxiety and Grief" by Christian Jarrett

"The Role of Visualization in Achieving Your Goals" by Psychology Today

"Mindfulness Meditation in Its Effects on the Brain" by Harvard Health Publishing

"How Breathing Calms Your Brain, and Other Science-Based Benefits of Controlled Breathing" by Forbes

The Mindful Path of Self- Compassion (Metta Prayer) – by Christopher Germer

"How Do Music Activities Affect Health and Well-Being? A Scoping Review of Studies Examining Psychosocial Mechanisms" (https://www.frontiersin.org/journals/psychology)
Chat GPT

Appendix C: Journaling Prompts and Exercises for Manifestation Practice

Here are journal prompts designed for a week of manifestation practice, incorporating gratitude affirmations, visualization, and Bible scriptures. These prompts are original and tailored for your book's appendix:

Journal Prompts for Manifestation Practice

Day 1: Gratitude Reflection

Prompt: List five things you are grateful for today. Reflect on how these blessings have positively impacted your life.

Affirmation: "I am grateful for the abundance that surrounds me."

Scripture: "Give thanks in all circumstances; for this is the Will of God in Christ Jesus for you" (1 Thessalonians 5:18).

Day 2: Visualization of Goals

Prompt: Close your eyes and visualize your most cherished goal as if it has already been achieved. Describe this vision in detail.

Affirmation: "I see my dreams manifesting in my reality."

Scripture: "For I know the plans I have for you, declares the Lord, plans to prosper you and not to harm you, plans to give you hope and a future" (Jeremiah 29:11).

Day 3: Affirmations of Self-Worth

Prompt: Write down three affirmations that reinforce your self-worth and potential. Repeat them daily.

Affirmation: "I am worthy of all the good life has to offer."

Scripture: "I praise you because I am fearfully and wonderfully made; your works are wonderful. I know that full well" (Psalm 139:14).

Day 4: Manifesting Abundance

Prompt: Reflect on what abundance means to you. Write about how you can invite more abundance into your life.

Affirmation: "Abundance flows effortlessly into my life."

Scripture: "And my God will meet all your needs according to the riches of his glory in Christ Jesus" (Philippians 4:19)

Day 5: Gratitude for Challenges

Prompt: Think of a recent challenge you faced. Write about what you learned from it and express gratitude for the growth it provided.

Affirmation: "I am grateful for the lessons that challenges bring."

Scripture: "Consider it pure joy, my brothers and sisters, whenever you face trials of many kinds" (James 1:2).

Day 6: Vision Board Creation

Prompt: Create a vision board (physically or digitally) representing your goals and dreams. Describe the images and words you choose.

Affirmation: "I manifest my desires with clarity and purpose."

Scripture: "Delight yourself in the Lord, and he will give you the desires of your heart" (Psalm 37:4).

Day 7: Reflection and Gratitude

Prompt: Review your journal entries from the week. Write about the feelings and insights you've gained through this practice.

Affirmation: "I am thankful for the journey of manifestation."

Scripture: "This is the day that the Lord has made; let us rejoice and be glad in it" (Psalm 118:24).

Final Thoughts

I want to extend my heartfelt gratitude for taking the time to read this book. If this is your first time reading it, or you read my first publication or other books, thank you! My prayer is that it blesses your life in such a profound way that you find yourself overflowing with gratitude for all the blessings you receive. I hope it brings positive transformation and deepens your connection with God, reminding you of His immense love and the goodness He desires for your life.

As you embark on your journey of manifestation, always remember that you are not alone. God's presence accompanies you, guiding and supporting you every step of the way. Embrace the principles and practices outlined in this book, remain steadfast in your goals, and trust in the divine plan that unfolds for you. Your path to manifestation reflects your faith, determination, and the incredible power of aligning your thoughts and actions with God's Word, scientific insights, and His Will. Remember, God's Word says in John 4:12, "Very truly I tell you, whoever believes in me will do the work I have been doing, and they will do even greater things than these, because I am going to the Father." The things you learned along the way are just programs that you can rewire for success. If there is one mantra I could impress on you that is biblical and science-proven to repeat often and daily, pray about everything (Philippians 4-6-7), lean not unto our own understanding (Proverbs 3:5-6), and do everything in love (1 Corinthians 16:14) to ourselves and others.

May your life be abundant with blessings, fulfilled and joyful as you continue to manifest your deepest desires in alignment with God's purpose. Keep your heart and mind open, maintain a positive outlook, and never underestimate the extraordinary power that God has bestowed upon you to create a life rich with purpose and happiness. It has been my greatest honor to share the insights that God has imparted to me over the years. Always remember you are a MASTERPIECE, AMAZING, ENOUGH, and WORTHY of a BLESSED, ABUNDANT LIFE! Share your newfound wisdom with others; together, we can heal the world. Reach out to me, and I will send you a link to a few free meditations you can use to boost your manifestation experience. Also, you can find out more about my Mastery Class - The Masterpiece Project. As always, Be Blessed and Be a Blessing! You can find other tools and resources on my website, social media, and YouTube channel.

Reflection Notes

Reflection Notes

About the Author

I possess a Master's Degree in Counseling Psychology and have invested over three decades in my career as a Licensed Counselor, Certified Brain Health Coach, Speaker, and Certified Health Integrative Medicine Professional. My expertise encompasses a broad spectrum of therapeutic approaches, such as Neurobiology, ADHD and Neurodiversity, Somatic Therapy, Energy Medicine, Neuro-Linguistic Programming (NLP), Cognitive Behavioral Therapy (CBT), Rational Emotive Therapy (RET), Emotional Freedom Techniques (EFT), Thought Field Therapy (TFT), Theology, Eye Movement Desensitization and Reprocessing (EMDR), the Gottman Method, alongside Mindfulness and Meditation. I am a multiple National and International Best-Selling Author and Speaker.

I am the owner of WarriorHeart Healing Hearts, where I champion a comprehensive healing philosophy that harmonizes the mind, body, and spirit using evidence based neuropsych tools and Bible scripture to rewire the brain for an abundantly blessed life.. I am the founder of the Masterpiece Project.. I help people clear up the mess to discover their MASTERPIECE! Over the years, I have had the honor of empowering thousands of individuals to heal, grow, glow, and soar!

Having faced my own set of adversities and emotional challenges, I understand that true healing flourishes within the framework of compassionate connections. Together, we nurture resilience and vitality, transforming our own legacies and those of future generations. Like iron sharpening iron, our collaboration fosters a profound healing journey. If you're looking for support or just want to connect, I'd love to hear from you! Be Blessed and Be a Blessing!

You can find more free resources to support you in your journey through the QR code.

https://msha.ke/warriorheartxo
https://linktr.ee/WarriorHeartxo
https://www.facebook.com/warriorheartxo
https://www.instagram.com/warriorheartxo
https://www.linkedin.com/in/erica-elliott-ms-lpc-b90911150

If *"Breath of Heaven: Manifesting God's Way"* has touched your life and helped you in any way, may I please ask a favor? I would be incredibly grateful if you could take a moment to leave a review. Your feedback not only helps me grow as an author but also plays a crucial role in getting my book into the hands of more readers to help them too.

When you leave a review, it helps my book be found more easily, allowing it to be placed in different categories where more people can discover it. Every review makes a difference, shining a light on my work, connecting others with the story that has touched you, and helping others draw closer to God. Let's share the blessings and expand this journey together!

All you have to do is go to Amazon by using the link below or by searching for my book title, *"Breath of Heaven: Manifesting God's Way."* Once there, simply click on five stars and write a review sharing what was helpful, impactful, or what you learned from the book. I'd love to hear how it has changed your thoughts on the Bible or your relationship with God. Your insights can inspire others and help them on their own journeys! Together we can change the world!

I can't wait to read your reviews! Thank you for your support!

Go to Author page and find the book to leave a review.
https://www.amazon.com/author/warriorheartxo